In my dreams I dance

In my dreams I dance

Anne Wafula Strike

A story of prejudice,
perseverance and pushing for change

HarperElement
An imprint of HarperCollins*Publishers*
1 London Bridge Street
London SE1 9GF

www.harpercollins.co.uk

HarperCollins*Publishers*
Macken House, 39/40 Mayor Street Upper
Dublin 1, D01 C9W8, Ireland

First published by HarperCollins 2010
This updated edition published 2024

1 3 5 7 9 10 8 6 4 2

A catalogue record of this book is
available from the British Library

ISBN 978-0-00-870301-1

Printed and bound in the UK using 100%
renewable electricity at CPI Group (UK) Ltd

MIX
Paper | Supporting
responsible forestry
FSC™ C007454

This book contains FSC™ certified paper and other controlled
sources to ensure responsible forest management.

For more information visit: www.harpercollins.co.uk/green

To Norman,
my son Timothy,
my dad George Paul Wafula
and Mama Florence

Contents

2024 Update

Prologue

'Get down! Get down!' barked the soldiers as they boarded the bus. Sweat dripped from their faces as they pointed their guns at us all. My heart was pounding, my mouth dry with fear and I was trembling from head to foot. I felt as if I was a character in a nightmarish action movie. The air was heavy with tension and the smell of stale sweat.

Many of the passengers obediently fell to their knees, sobbing and shaking hysterically. The soldiers were pushing down those who were too slow.

'Please don't shoot us! Put the guns away, we beg you,' a few of the women murmured. I could hear some people whispering prayers for deliverance.

I started screaming hysterically. I was just 13 years old and had never been so terrified in all my life.

'Get down, young girl,' the soldiers said, turning their guns on me. All I could do was look back at them, too frozen with fear to explain why I couldn't lie on the floor like the other passengers. Helplessly, I pointed to my callipers and crutches and hoped they would understand. Strapping and unstrapping the callipers took about ten minutes, so there was no way I could get down quickly.

The soldiers glanced at the callipers, but kept their guns trained on me.

It was August 1982 and we'd just pulled into the bus station in Nairobi. Everything was happening in slow motion. I felt as if eternity had passed since the soldiers boarded the bus, although in reality it wasn't more than a few moments.

I searched frantically through the bus windows for my dad. He had promised my teachers that he would be waiting to collect me. At that very moment he hurried onto the bus. I was shocked to see that he was carrying a black machine gun and was wearing many magazines of bullets. Although I'd seen him in his army uniform many times before, I'd never seen him armed and ready for action like this.

'Stop pointing those guns at my little girl!' he shouted at the soldiers. They hurriedly lowered them.

In a lightning flash my dad picked me up and put me over his shoulder. Holding me with one hand and his gun with the other, he gestured to one of the soldiers to carry my crutches and bag.

'What's happening, Dad? Please tell me what's happening!'

'I'm going to take you somewhere where you'll be safe, Anne,' he said briskly. 'We're in the middle of a coup. I'll explain everything to you when things have calmed down. Come, we must hurry, things are very bad in the streets.'

I wished he would put his scary gun and bullets down and take me home.

Before I could utter another word, he started running. As we hurried through the streets, I heard people calling out, 'Run for your lives!'

My dad put a coat over my head to shield my eyes. But I had already seen some of the horror.

I started to cry.

Chapter One

Walking and Running

You have to travel through the Great Rift Valley to reach the village where I was born. It's a small place called Mihuu in western Kenya, about 500 kilometres from the capital, Nairobi. Only a few hundred people live there and it has little more than a modest market and a mill to grind maize. The nearest town is Webuye, one of the stations on the main rail line from Kampala, in Uganda, to Nairobi. Webuye is surrounded by the steep, rocky Chetambe Hills, and Mihuu, with its rich, fertile soil, nestles behind those hills. The red volcanic earth is good for growing many crops – millet, sorghum, bananas and sugarcane. Life is tuned to the rhythm of the seasons – everything revolves around planting, weeding and harvesting.

I was born on 8 May 1969 in a mud hut. My grandmother and many of my female relatives were there to help me into the world.

'This one has come out more easily than the others, even though she's the heaviest,' my mum said, sighing with relief.

The women gathered round to coo over the new arrival. My grandmother cradled me in her arms and said, 'This child is a real beauty and she's slipped into the world so easily, she's a blessing on us all. I'm sure she won't give you any trouble in life.'

My mum's friend Annah, a wonderful singer, had sung to me while I was in the womb. She had held my mum's stomach and said, 'This child is going to be great.' My mum and dad named me Annah after her and this was later changed to Anne. My African name is Naliaka, which means 'born during the weeding season'.

The language spoken in the village is Luhya, which is also the name of a big tribe in the region. My family belongs to the Bukusu clan, a section of the Luhya tribe.

I'm the fourth born of eight. First came Alice, then Kennedy, Jane, me, Evans and Victoria, who are twins, Goddard and Geoffrey. I also have three step-siblings, Irene, Melvin and Arthur. Kennedy, my oldest brother, was named after the US President Kennedy. My dad said he hoped he would rise up and be at least as great as Kennedy. Evans' middle name is Lincoln, after Abraham Lincoln, and Victoria was named after Queen Victoria. Geoffrey was named after Geoffrey de Freitas, a British ambassador who became a Labour MP. Goddard was named after a British judge my dad admired.

My dad started life as a Muslim, Athumani Wafula, but later converted to Christianity and changed his name to George Paul. He is a very well educated man and has always had a mind wide open to new challenges and ideas. He has always understood the possibilities the world holds for his children and has pushed us to strive to be the best we can possibly be. He admires the British way of doing things and is very well read in British and American history. He is a very fair, loving and upstanding man. I couldn't wish for better.

When I was born he was a warrant officer in the Kenyan African Rifles and it was more than a month before he was able to return home to see me.

'I was hoping for a son,' he said, grinning and looking lovingly into my eyes. 'But I'm just as happy to have a girl. She's so beautiful.'

'Yes, this one is the strongest of all our babies,' my mum said proudly.

My mum was called Nekesa Ruth. Nekesa means 'born during the harvesting season'. With Kenyan names, people can roughly guess when your birthday is.

My mother's parents were very devout Quakers. My mum herself was a friendly and generous person and also strikingly beautiful. My dad often tells me that he fell in love with her as soon as he saw her and asked her parents there and then if he could marry her.

Our home was simple, but to us it was beautiful. The floor and walls were made of mud and cow dung, and a certain type of reed that grew near the river made a cool and shady roof. We had five rooms, so it was quite a grand place by village standards. We had no electricity, but used kerosene lamps to read by in the evening. Our entertainment was a radio and a battery-operated record player. We listened to Voice of Kenya, which began its broadcasts at 5.55 every morning.

My dad played lots of old Motown records and early James Brown. I still remember my older brother and sisters and my cousins wearing bell bottoms and plat-forms in an attempt to look like the singers on the record covers and dancing to the soul routines. We younger ones weren't allowed to join in, but we used to peep through the door, enviously looking at them having fun. We would also make up words in Swahili that sounded about the same as the English words.

Life in the village was very traditional, with people looking after their animals and cultivating small pieces of land. A father would share his land with his sons and it would be passed down the generations. At that time people grew just enough food to feed their families and took very little to market to sell. But now things are slowly starting to change. Increasingly, sugarcane is grown to sell because it fetches a good price. My dad used to grow maize, cassava, potatoes and bananas, but now he, too, is growing sugarcane.

When I was a child, food was always plentiful because my mum and my grandmother were out working hard in the fields. Any surplus was given to our neighbours.

Sharing, especially of food, is a concept deeply ingrained in African life.

Water was collected from the river in a very organised way. There was one part of the river where the water was pure enough for drinking and another part where clothes were washed and the animals would drink. It's the same today.

When I was born many children in the village didn't go to school. But for my dad education was a priority. He had trained as a teacher before he joined the army and he valued learning for its own sake as well as a passport to a better life. 'Education is the key to everything,' he would often say, and he encouraged all of us to learn at every opportunity.

He also loved imparting knowledge to me and my brothers and sisters. He used to read a lot and was particularly impressed with the history of ancient Greece and the strength of its people. He explained to us that all the strong sportspeople used to gather at Mount Olympus. Because I was such a strong and healthy child when I was born, he gave me Olympia as a middle name. He thought this would suit me. Even as a small baby, if I kicked against his stomach when he picked me up, he said he could really feel the power of my foot.

'Olympia is a good name for you,' he told me. 'You are going to be a very strong and special girl. I believe you will achieve great things.'

* * *

Tradition was a very important part of life for our clan, as it is to this day. Bukusus believe in many things that Westerners would find strange. Most of the people who have never been to school believe in black magic. They call it 'African science'. When someone has died mysteriously, people say, 'Oh, we think African science was involved.'

When I was just a few months old, the women from our family went out to our farm. It was the harvesting season, Nekesa. My mum placed me carefully under the shade of a tree on an animal skin and some cloth. A little while later she came to check on me and screamed in horror: a black mamba was coiled around me.

These snakes are common in our village. Once my grandmother walked all the way back from the bush to the village with one wrapped in her bundle of firewood. She felt something tapping her on the back and thought it was one of the branches, but when she got home she discovered it was in fact a lethal snake. She carefully unloaded her bundle and called on someone in the village to kill the snake.

Faced with a snake wrapped around her precious baby, my mum fell to her knees and, with tears rolling down her cheeks, started begging the snake, 'Please leave my child alone.'

My grandmother walked up calmly and hushed her. 'This snake would have killed the baby by now if that's what it wanted to do,' she said quietly. She started praying softly and whispering something under her breath.

The snake was obviously listening, because it lazily uncoiled itself and slithered away, leaving me unharmed. The tree where I lay is still there today.

At the time there was an old woman in the village who had a reputation as a witch, and the villagers started whispering that she had sent the snake to curse me because she was envious of my strength and beauty. No one could understand how I had survived such a thing unscathed.

In many ways I was a very lucky child. I was happy, lively, healthy, tall for my age and by the time I was nine months old I was already running around. Unlike my brothers and sisters, I'd never even needed to have any herbs gathered in the bush and boiled to cure various ills. In the first two-and-a-half years of my life, as I scampered around energetically on the soft earth, exploring my village and learning new words every day, none of us had any idea of the shadow that was about to descend.

Chapter Two

The Day My Life Changed

I was too young to remember what happened next, but my family have told me the terrible story many times. As swiftly as a rainy season downpour drenches the earth, my happy, carefree life in the village ended.

My dad was away trying to stop the Shiftas, Somalian bandits, from crossing the border into Kenya and stealing livestock, when catastrophe struck. I had accompanied my mum to the river. As usual she was washing clothes and then washing us. I liked to carry a small pot of water on my head, copying the huge pot she balanced effortlessly on hers. But something was wrong with me that day. As soon as we returned to the homestead, I fell down screaming.

My family thought a snake had bitten me, even though none had been seen anywhere near me. But, after examining my writhing body all over, my grandmother, who was an expert in these things, pronounced, 'No snake has bitten this child.'

My mum and grandmother could see that I was in terrible pain, but if it wasn't a snake, what had caused it? They had no idea. Nor could they calm my screams. They told me later that I had cried for 24 hours, giving great heaving dry sobs when no more tears would come. At one point I was so distressed, I swallowed my tongue. And then my whole body went limp.

My grandmother was a Christian, so she prayed and poured holy water over me. When that didn't work, she turned to traditional medicines. She was perplexed. Why was a previously healthy child suddenly unable to talk or eat? How could it be that I had gone down to the river apparently well and had returned terribly ill?

The more baffled everybody became, the more desperate the remedies they resorted to. My legs were massaged with donkey dung, tribal cuts were carved into my skin and foul-tasting potions were forced down my throat. Though my dad was an educated man, he too believed that the herbs could cure me because a British doctor had once told him that a lot of powerful Western medicines were contained in them.

Alas, none of the traditional remedies did me any good. My condition was deteriorating and I was struggling to breathe. My family were convinced they were going to lose me.

In a flash of inspiration, one of the villagers found a plastic tube and put it into my mouth. Family and friends took turns blowing their breath into me to keep me alive. It was the primitive equivalent of an iron lung.

After a few weeks I recovered enough to breathe unaided, but my breathing remained very laboured and the bottom half of my body mysteriously withered, leaving me unable to move around. I was effectively paralysed from the neck down. I reverted to babyhood, no longer able to talk or to stop myself from dribbling. I shared a bed with my mum and she had to turn me over when I wanted to change position. With tears in her eyes, she fed me sloppy food because I could no longer chew anything. Her lively, inquisitive daughter had turned into a helpless rag doll.

'What kind of illness is this?' my mum and my grandmother kept asking each other. They had never seen anything like it before.

My immediate and extended family rallied round, but some of the villagers thought I'd been cursed and should be left to die.

Solomon, a local witch doctor, was called in to treat me, but he too drew a blank, muttering only that an evil spell had been cast on me. 'This is caused by black magic,' he declared.

People in the village started to shun our family. 'They've been struck by a curse from God,' they muttered. They couldn't understand my parents' determination to keep me alive. 'She's more or less dead – let her complete her dying,' they said.

My dad didn't discover what had happened to me until he returned home on leave six weeks later. He was distraught at this terrible transformation in his formerly healthiest child. 'We're not going to give up on our daughter,' he said firmly whenever the villagers urged him to let me die.

So profound was his distress that he even forgot to shave when he went back to the army. Shaving regularly was a vital part of army discipline, but he told his superiors that he hadn't bothered because it 'wasn't important'. He was promptly demoted for rudeness and lost out on being commissioned as a senior officer. My illness was not only affecting me but also those I loved the most.

Gradually some movement returned to my upper body, although from the waist down it remained like dead wood. Slowly and painfully I learned to pull myself onto my stomach, my thin misshapen legs and feet dangling inertly, and drag myself along the floor using my arms.

My mum and dad were delighted that I had regained some mobility, but this technique didn't impress the villagers. 'There's a young snake living in that house,' they chorused. 'It is not right that it should remain amongst us.' They gathered at our door and said, 'You need to get rid of that child, otherwise the curse that has possessed her will spread to the other children in the village.'

My mum begged and pleaded with them to leave us in peace, but they were in no mood to compromise.

'We're going to burn your house down,' they informed her. 'It's better that you leave now, before you all perish.'

Family members advised my mum to run away and we escaped to my maternal grandparents' home in a nearby village. We stayed there until my dad was next home on leave.

The behaviour of the villagers made him sad and angry. 'We have as much right as anyone else to live in our own village,' he said. 'This is our ancestral land.'

Defiantly, he rebuilt our home, substituting corrugated iron for straw so that the villagers couldn't burn it down. But even with the reinforcements we continued to feel under siege.

My dad was confused by my illness. He had a modern, educated outlook but was also steeped in the traditions of the village and wasn't entirely sure if my illness was a new disease or witchcraft.

He was also torn between staying at home to protect his family and continuing in the military so that he could pay for our schooling and give us the kind of life he had ambitions to provide for us.

Eventually, with a heavy heart, he decided to apply for accommodation in the army barracks in Nairobi for all the family. He thought that we would encounter less prejudice in the capital and hoped that I would be able to get some proper medical treatment there. He also thought that that way he could be closer to us.

His faith in me remained steadfast. 'One way or another you're going to recover, Anne,' he said. 'The local remedies haven't worked, but in Nairobi you can get the most modern treatments.'

It was very hard for my dad to uproot his entire family and transplant us all into unfamiliar territory, but he felt he had no choice. He realised he wasn't going to succeed in changing attitudes in the village and needed to keep his family safe.

So, one year after my illness started, our family gathered up our belongings and bade farewell to the villagers. Our relatives cried, but it was clear that many other people were glad to see the back of us.

In many ways it was a relief to my family to make a new start and our mood as we travelled to Nairobi on the JJ Family bus was quite positive. My mum and dad took turns at holding me on their lap.

The first thing my dad did after we'd settled in was to take me to Kenyatta hospital where I could be examined by a proper doctor. The hospital was overcrowded, dirty and chaotic and overflowing at the seams with people of all ages suffering from everything from malaria to malnutrition.

The doctor examined me carefully, moving my limbs in various directions and noting the shape of my spine.

My family gathered around anxiously. They hoped not only for a diagnosis but also a cure, so that the lively two-and-a-half year old who had suddenly been lost to them could at last be restored to full health.

Although my condition was a mystery to my family, the inhabitants of my village and assorted witch doctors, it wasn't to the doctor at Kenyatta hospital. He looked at my body flapping helplessly like a fish on the shore and pronounced flatly, 'This is polio.'

My mum and dad gasped.

I was too young to understand what was going on and lay oblivious to the sickening blow the doctor had just delivered.

'But all my children have been vaccinated against polio,' my dad said. 'My wife walked many miles to the health clinic with Anne to make sure she had the vaccine.'

Some Kenyans chose not to vaccinate their offspring because they thought that whatever substance those strange syringes were putting into children's bodies was a plan of the white man to reduce the African population. My family, however, didn't share that view.

The doctor shrugged. 'That's too bad. But it happens sometimes. Maybe the vaccine was out of date and not that effective.'

He explained that the polio virus had attacked my spine, entering in an asymmetrical way and leaving it curved in two places. Some muscles had completely wasted away, though some function remained in others.

'What can you do for her?' my dad asked.

'I'm sorry, there is nothing we can do for her now,' said the doctor, shaking his head sadly. 'She can have some physiotherapy to improve the movement in the muscles that are still working and a plaster cast to straighten out the limbs, but we can't restore movement. We can't repair the nerves the virus has destroyed.'

My mum started to cry. My dad put his arm around her and did his best to comfort her.

Polio is a virus carried in water and food that causes nerve damage. It attacks different parts of the body, leaving them withered and lifeless. There is a great deal of knowledge about how to prevent it now, but because it has been successfully eradicated in most of the world it is regarded as a disease of the past and not one that researchers are looking into anymore.

As I lay quietly on the examination table my dad sighed heavily, wondering what kind of life lay ahead for me. One thing was certain though: things were not going to be easy.

Still, he was determined to try to make the best of it. 'Well, thank God my daughter has survived,' he said. 'We will find a way to make life as good as possible for her.' He stroked my hair sadly. 'You are a strong girl, Anne, and I know that somehow you will overcome all of this. I didn't give you the middle name Olympia for nothing. I know that despite your polio you will still show the world how strong and powerful you are.'

I didn't understand what he was talking about and was absorbed in looking at the strange surroundings of the hospital, a place that looked nothing like the traditional village I had spent all of my life in. Things were already changing for me.

* * *

Our family moved into Kahawa barracks and without any fuss adapted to my newly diagnosed disability. My dad was given a small two-roomed place which was more luxurious than our home in the village because it was made of stone and had running water and electricity. My mum lavished enormous care and attention on me. Because she couldn't do farming in Nairobi, she spent much more time doing knitting and needlework and completely devoted herself to her children. I lacked for nothing and she knew instinctively everything that I needed in order to thrive. She made sure I was always clean and comfortable and played with me a lot. My favourite foods were beans and sweet potatoes with fermented milk, mixed with dried leaves and mashed together into a thick paste. She often cooked this for me because she knew how much I loved it.

One of the best things about our new life was that nobody wanted to burn our house down anymore. Nobody living in the barracks pronounced that our family was cursed because of my disability.

Back in the village, our extended family took over the farming of my dad's land so that we didn't have to worry about it being neglected.

The doctors at Kenyatta hospital referred me to an orthopaedic hospital, Kabete, on the outskirts of Nairobi. The doctors there were very familiar with cases like mine and, as the doctor at Kenyatta hospital had predicted, put me in a heavy, uncomfortable plaster cast from my feet to halfway up my ribcage with just a space between my legs to allow me to urinate and defecate. I was very floppy and my knees and elbows were starting to bend. The doctors said that the plaster would straighten my muscles and help me to grow to a normal height. You see some polio survivors in Africa whose knees are bent permanently because they were not put into plaster.

'I know it will be hard for you to put up with the plaster, Anne, but this is the best chance you have to straighten out your twisted body,' the doctors explained.

I had to endure this for about a year, which would be hard enough for an adult but was particularly tough for a little girl like me. I couldn't understand why my body was suddenly locked into this horrible white material. In the village I'd adapted well to only being able to use the top half of my body, but being trapped inside the plaster often made me cry. It was the worst kind of prison and always became unbearably itchy. A new cast was put on every three months and each time the medical staff removed the old plaster they found many wounds underneath it where I had managed to dig my finger or a spoon through the plaster to scratch the maddening itches. Sometimes lice got under my plaster and bred there in the warm conditions.

While I was in the cast my mum carried me around everywhere. My sisters Alice and Jane were very good to me and found ways to adapt their games so that I could join in. We liked to play a game with bottle tops where the person who could make the tallest pile was the winner. My hands used to shake a lot and my sisters helped me to steady them as I tried to place one bottle top over another. Unwittingly, they were helping with my rehabilitation.

The hospital staff always used a noisy saw to remove the old plaster and its harsh screech made me cry, but afterwards my body felt so free. I was allowed a few plaster-free days before the new plaster was applied. At these times one of my sisters would fling me onto her back. It was much easier for my family to carry me around when I was plaster-free.

To me the plaster was just a heavy burden – I couldn't understand the advantage of it at all. Sometimes I poured ink from my dad's fountain pen onto it so that it didn't look boring plain white. My sisters helped me decorate it. We giggled over the designs we created and it made the whole thing a little bit easier for me to bear. When I got bored I would pick up sharp sticks and make chipped patterns in the plaster. Whether I liked it or not, it was part of me and so I just had to find ways to live with it.

My mum and dad did their best to stay cheerful, but both were devastated by my condition. Every time they looked at me they saw the happy, active child I had been before the virus had struck. Seeing their little girl struggle with a partially paralysed body caused them great pain.

'Your sickness is like a knife going through my heart,' my dad would often say sadly.

* * *

My mum and dad were members of the Pentecostal Assemblies of God and when I arrived at church with my mum, the people said, 'Let that crippled child come forward and we will pray for her.'

Reluctantly my mum took me to the front of the church, where a group of congregants shook me hard and pulled my legs. I can still remember the agony of that pulling.

'Don't cry, child. We're trying to cast out the demons in your body,' they said.

'Leave the poor girl alone,' my mum said. 'She has suffered enough.'

She and my dad were very unhappy with the church for the attitude they adopted towards me. But both were devout Christians, so they continued to attend services there.

When my mum returned to the village for a visit she encountered similar attitudes. Even though we were no longer living there, people wanted to come to our house to pray for the demons inside me to be cast out. They told my mum she needed to slaughter goats and sacrifice them if she wanted me to get better, but my mum and dad refused to get involved with these superstitious rituals.

'Our daughter has polio and she's trying to get help,' my mum said firmly.

Although we didn't encounter problems in the barracks, there was plenty of prejudice in Nairobi too. My brother and sisters faced abuse because of my disability when they attended school. 'Our parents say we shouldn't play with you because your sister is a cripple and you will bring bad luck to us,' their schoolfriends said. But they ignored their jibes, loyally defending me and doing their best to protect me. They carried me on their backs to wherever they were going to play and put me down nearby so that I could be part of what was going on. When they climbed trees to pick fruit, they made sure they threw some down for me to eat.

My brother was often busy playing football with the other boys or killing animals or birds with a slingshot, so I didn't get too involved with his games, but Alice, Jane and I often played together. To them, I wasn't a girl with a disability, but simply their sister Anne.

My dad gave me the pet name Mamy, a term of love and respect, and my mum did everything for me – bathing me, wiping my bottom and putting me to bed, helped by my brother and sisters. No child could have been more loved and cherished by their family than I was by mine.

My family became very sensitive to my difficulties, but not all of my relatives understood my condition so well. I used to have long hair and one of my earliest memories is of sitting uncomfortably on the knee of an aunt while she plaited my hair in cornrows. Sitting in that position caused me great pain and I began to cry.

'That girl's body is aching all over. Don't hurt her more by plaiting her hair,' my dad said.

Although at that time I wasn't fully aware that I was disabled, I was aware that I was different from other children and my parents spent a lot of time reassuring me. They told me that I was a beautiful, intelligent girl who would succeed in life. 'Don't listen to what anyone else says. You're beautiful on the inside and the outside and everything will be fine,' my dad often said. 'Your middle name is Olympia and your destiny is to be great.'

When he returned home at the end of the day he always called out, 'Where is my rose flower?'

My heart lifted when I heard him utter those words.

When I first went to Kabete I didn't pay too much attention to the other patients, but by the time I was four I began to notice that there were others like me at the centre. I became friendly with a little girl called Rosa who also had polio and we used to play together at the hospital.

When I was four-and-a-half years old the staff at Kabete decided that I didn't need to be in plaster any longer. The day I heard that news I clapped my hands together and whooped with joy. I thought that at long last my body would be left in peace. For a few months, it was. But my relief was short-lived.

'It's time to fit you with some callipers, Anne,' the staff told me. I'd no idea what they were talking about, but I didn't like the sound of it.

I cried when I was fitted with my first pair of callipers and crutches. They felt almost as restrictive as the plaster. I felt cheated. I had simply exchanged one prison for another.

The aim of the callipers was to keep my legs straight and help me to walk, but I could only wear them for an hour at a time at first because they hurt me so much. They were clamped to the whole of my legs, with an extension for the lower part of my ribcage. The metal was held to my legs with leather straps. The whole contraption was very hot and uncomfortable, totally impractical for use in a hot African country.

My right leg was a few inches shorter than the left and I was given ugly black polio boots to wear, one a few inches higher than the other to balance my uneven legs. I hated wearing these boots almost as much as wearing the callipers. I looked longingly at the other children of my age who ran around barefoot or in flip flops.

I did enjoy the gentle, relaxing physiotherapy treatment on offer at Kabete, but sometimes the physiotherapists pulled my tendons to stretch my legs and it was so painful that I used to scream. I grew to hate doctors in white coats and associated them only with pain. I tried to accept my situation, but I had reached an age where all I wanted was to be like the other children who ran around the barracks in nothing more than a few flimsy clothes.

Chapter Three

Joyland

When I was four-and-a-half years old my dad found out about a boarding school for children with disabilities called Joyland School for the Physically Handicapped and decided that that would be the best possible place for me to go. English missionaries from the Salvation Army ran the school and the standard of education was said to be very high there. For my dad the school combined his love of education and of all things English, so he was delighted when I secured a place there.

There were actually two schools – one in Thika, near Nairobi, and one in Kisumu, about four hours' drive from our village. It was decided that I would attend the latter.

I was devastated when my dad broke the news to me. I was used to being close to my mum day and night and the idea of being separated from her was too much to bear. My mum did everything for me – how would I survive without her? And how would I manage without my sisters? I was sure that nobody else would be able to play games so well with me.

'Please don't make me go. I'm scared. I can't manage without all of you,' I sobbed. I was surrounded by love and suddenly that love was going to be snatched away from me.

'You can come home every three months for the school holidays,' my dad said.

I had no concept of how long three months would last for, but I didn't like the sound of it at all. And I didn't want to be away from my family for even one day.

But my dad insisted. 'You know I only have your best interests at heart, Anne,' he said, stroking my hand. However much I cried, he remained determined I should go to school.

Finally the day dawned and my mum and dad took me to Kisumu on the bus. I sobbed throughout the journey and my mum spent all her time trying to hush me and wipe away my tears.

'This school will be very good for you,' she said, 'and you'll be coming home in the holidays, so we won't be apart for too long. We are fortunate, too, that the Salvation Army makes no charge to attend the school.'

I wasn't convinced.

'I'm expecting great things from you, Anne,' my dad said gently, 'and how will you achieve in life if you don't go to school? We're lucky to have found such a nice school for you. They are used to looking after children like you and your life will be much easier for you than at an ordinary school. You won't have to struggle here and so you can really concentrate on getting a good education.'

'I don't care about my education, I just want to be at home with all of you,' I said.

Nothing my parents said could console me and when we arrived at the school my face was crumpled from so much crying. My dad carried me through the gates and then put me down in the grounds.

I became hysterical because I knew that I was about to be parted from my mum and dad.

Also, the school looked huge to me. I'd never seen anything like it. It was much worse than I'd expected. I'd thought maybe it would be a little school, not a massive place like this. I was sure I'd get lost all the time. And how would I ever be able to walk across the enormous grounds in my crutches and callipers? I could see some of the staff and older children walking around and they all looked like giants compared with me.

Joyland was actually a modern, sturdy building surrounded by beautiful gardens and everything about it was peaceful and well ordered, but even if it had been an exact replica of paradise it wouldn't have impressed me at that moment. I clung to my mum's legs and started to wail. I couldn't imagine life without the woman who lovingly catered for my every need.

Some of the staff members came to greet us and advised my parents that it would be best if they left so that I could get used to my new life.

My mum and dad hugged me and whispered once more that I'd be home for the holidays very soon.

'Please don't leave me,' I begged, but they walked away.

Feeling completely bereft, I stared helplessly at their disappearing backs. I felt completely lost and alone. How could my parents abandon me like that?

I looked around in absolute bewilderment. I was surrounded by strangers.

Then one of them, a well-built, bubbly woman with very short hair, came up to me.

'I'm Mama Salome,' she said, beaming. 'I'm the house mother for your dormitory. I'm going to bring a wheel-chair to take you to the place where you'll be sleeping.'

I didn't know what she was talking about. I didn't know what a wheelchair was and I didn't know that as well as teachers, Joyland employed house mothers, who were, as the name suggests, substitutes for our own mothers.

A few minutes later Mama Salome returned with the chair. I had never seen a chair like that with big wheels attached to it, but I was relieved when she lifted me into it. I was still struggling to get used to my callipers and crutches and it was hard for me to stand up or walk for any length of time. I was exhausted from the journey and all the crying, and desperately wanted to lie down and go to sleep so that I could block out this strange world I was suddenly alone in.

'We only have two wheelchairs,' Mama Salome explained, 'so we use them as taxis to ferry around all the children who have difficulty walking. Sometimes we squeeze two or three children at a time into a chair.'

I had already noticed that some of the children could walk without assistance, although others relied on callipers and crutches to get around.

Mama Salome showed me where the spotlessly clean bathrooms were and demonstrated how the flushing toilets and showers worked. I was terrified by the sound of the flushing and the ferocious splashing of the water from the shower. Later I discovered that many of the children were so frightened by these strange contraptions that the first time they saw them they ran away.

At home my mum had washed me using a bucket of water. I hadn't been able to use the traditional long drop toilet – simply a deep hole dug into the earth – so she had allowed me to defecate onto a piece of paper that she then took outside to the long drop. Here, because the toilets were so clean and there were no stairs to navigate, the children could easily crawl on their hands and knees to them, something that would have been very unpleasant at a long drop toilet. All the facilities at the school were designed to make life as easy as possible for children with physical disabilities.

Next I was shown the place where I was sleeping, which Mama Salome explained was called a dormitory.

I had never seen such a big room for sleeping in before, nor so many beds lined up in neat rows. They looked very comfortable, but I couldn't lie down and sleep yet.

Next Mama Salome offered to help me unpack. She folded the clothes that my mum had packed for me, but then started scratching her head.

'Where is your underwear, Anne?' she asked. 'There doesn't seem to be any here.'

At first I didn't know what she was talking about and felt very embarrassed that I hadn't brought something with me that was apparently important.

At home I had always worn trousers and it had made life easier not to wear any underwear. At Joyland, though, all children had to wear underwear underneath their uniform of brown tunics or trousers and yellow blouses or shirts.

'Never mind. I'm sure we can find something for you,' Mama Salome said kindly. 'Come, I'll show you around a bit more.'

Joyland was surrounded by a wire fence. The staff room, library and Salvation Army major's house were all close to the main gate. There was also a nursery school and I saw young children there wearing the tiniest callipers and crutches. I soon discovered that they were taught independence from a very early age.

There was a tailoring room where uniforms were made to fit each child, because many of the children did not fit standard clothes. Those with curved spines or misshapen limbs were given specially made clothes that fitted perfectly and felt very comfortable.

All the buildings were surrounded by well-tended flowerbeds. 'The more able-bodied children look after these,' Mama Salome explained.

After all the events of the day, I was relieved when it was finally time to crawl into bed. I was used to sharing a bed with my mum or my sisters and it felt strange and lonely having a whole bed to myself. I missed the warm bodies and breath of the members of my family as I drifted off to sleep.

The next morning I began to learn about how things worked at Joyland. The school day was highly structured, unlike life at home, which was much more laid-back.

The house mothers woke us up at the same time every day. When I first arrived Mama Salome helped me to get dressed, as I was unable to manage this by myself, but the emphasis was on teaching us to become independent.

I was allowed to have breakfast in the dormitory at first, as I was unable to get to the dining room, but before long I managed the journey on my crutches and callipers and joined the others.

Our meals always followed a similar pattern – porridge for breakfast, maize and beans for lunch, and *ugali* for supper, a form of maize with vegetables. We were also given tinned salmon and tuna regularly and I grew to love eating them. The only fish I had tasted before was tilapia. We were given a big chunk of cheese three times a week and at first I thought it tasted like soap and used to trade it for fish. Eventually, though, I developed a taste for it.

Whenever I cried because I was missing my family, Mama Salome put her arms around me and said, 'Don't cry, my child, you and all the other children are here so that you can have a better life.'

She knew all the children in her dormitory very well and made sure all of us were well cared for and happy. She had a little bedsit next to our beds where she cooked her own food.

Although the children at Joyland had all sorts of disabilities, we were all equal and nobody stared at anyone else as if they were a freak. Whatever the disability, everyone fitted in. There were plenty of children who had been disabled by polio as well as those with conditions like cerebral palsy. Some children used to dribble and were unable to talk, but the staff found a way to make sure they joined in with everybody else.

A lot of love and care went into supporting us and as the weeks went by I stopped crying and actually began to enjoy myself. The physical longing to return home began to subside, although I still missed my family very much. The environment was comfortable, stimulating and much more suited to people with disabilities than the barracks in Nairobi. More importantly, I was surrounded by kindness. I began to realise that the school's name was an accurate one – it really was a land full of joy.

I grew to appreciate the calm order and superb facilities at the school. There was a swimming pool and a gym for rehabilitation. I cried the first time they tried to get me to go into the swimming pool, though, because I thought it was like the river in our village at home, which was full of snakes and crocodiles lying in wait. Eventually the staff managed to explain to me that it was safe to get into the pool.

The gym was an empty hall furnished only with mats to lie down on and some walking rails. A physiotherapist who knew what kind of movements would benefit our limbs taught us what was called PE but was more like rehabilitation. She used to place me gently on my back, remove my callipers and try to stretch my legs. The more able children threw a ball at each other. However severe a child's disability, the teachers and physiotherapists made sure everyone was included in these sessions.

We were placed in different dormitories according to our ages. There were four boys' dormitories on one side of the site and four girls' dormitories on the other side. The lights were switched off at 8 p.m. sharp and until that time we sang our hearts out.

Mama Salome often taught us new songs – hymns and traditional African songs – and encouraged us to compose our own music. As we sang she said, 'If God is looking down from heaven right now, He will be so pleased with all of you.'

As part of the drive to make us self-sufficient we were taught how to wash our own clothes. Often we didn't do a good job and the house mothers had to rewash them for us, but at least we tried. We were also taught how to fold our clothes and make our beds, and doing both quickly became a habit.

At home we all used tree bark to clean our teeth, but at school I was given two alien things instead – a toothbrush and toothpaste. At first I hated the feel of the brush and the minty taste of the toothpaste, but I soon got used to it and found I preferred it to tree bark.

Lessons were 35 minutes long. I loved Swahili, English and music, but hated mathematics, and also art, because I couldn't draw. The standard of teaching was very high. A lot of money had gone into the school and the missionaries wanted to make sure we did well academically. We followed the same curriculum as other Kenyan schoolchildren, but we had some British textbooks and our education was a mix of Kenyan teaching and that of different European countries like England and Holland, where some of the Salvation Army people came from.

The headmaster was a man called Sammy, who was very popular with all the children. He put a lot of effort into making us all laugh. In the middle of an apparently serious conversation he would climb up onto the desks and dance. It was impossible to feel cross about anything when we watched Sammy performing. He used to make up songs for me about how much my dad loved me and that made me feel really good.

I was in a class with children of all different ages –
some children didn't start at Joyland until they were a
few years older than me but had to start in the first class
because they had never received any education before.

At first I hated having to go to lessons. All I wanted
to do was play with my dollies like any other girl of my
age, but I soon overcame my dislike of the lessons and
began to soak up the information my teachers gave me. I
swelled with pride when I won an award for my handwriting.

To begin with I was very nervous in maths lessons,
but once I learned to relax I began to do well. I even
managed to bring about a change in our teacher's
approach to learning. He was extremely strict and caned
us if we failed the tests he set us, even though the school
policy was not to cane the children. When I failed one
test I fell on the floor crying, asked to use the toilet and
then locked myself in to avoid being caned. I refused to
come out until the end of the lesson. When the Salvation
Army bosses heard about this, they were furious with
the teacher and made sure that he stopped caning children. He was unhappy about the ban and was scornful
about the white people, who he said were 'too soft'.

I started to do well in all my subjects and wondered if
my dad's prediction about my middle name Olympia
really would come true one day. For the first time in my
life, I started to feel successful.

I also made friends at Joyland. One was called Abigail.
She was a few years older than me and was in one of the

dormitories for the older girls. She was a lovely friendly girl who wanted to make sure that everyone was happy. She made me feel safe and protected.

I was also friendly with two girls called Monica and Grace. We would sit outside together playing with our dollies and giggling. We tried to do knitting with sticks and grass and fell about laughing at our rather poor attempts.

I still felt very homesick and sometimes I burst into tears when I thought about my mum and everyone else at home.

'Don't cry, Anne,' said Monica. 'You can have my dolly, that will make you feel better.'

'And have my book too,' said Grace, putting her arms around me and trying to wipe my tears away.

I still missed home, but my friends certainly made me feel more comfortable at school.

My best friend was a girl called Sarah. She had the luxury of one fully functioning leg and we all thought she was extremely able. Sometimes she stood up and danced for us or proudly walked for a short distance without the calliper that supported her bad leg. She was able to wear sandals and as I stared at my heavy polio boots I was very envious of her.

Generally, all the children got along well together. Of course we sometimes had disagreements and insulted each other, but like quick-drying showers these fallouts didn't last for long. The emphasis on singing really bound us together as a group. We sometimes entered singing competitions, competing against able-bodied schools, and to our immense delight we always won.

One of the unexpected pleasures about Joyland was the library. I had learned my ABC from my family before going to school, but to begin with I couldn't read. I started off using colouring books containing cut-out dolls and a cut-out range of outfits for them to wear. I also loved looking at books containing pictures of other countries.

The library was full of European books, along with a few Kenyan ones. Once I had learned to read, I read the children's books over and over again. *Jack and the Beanstalk* was one of my favourites. We weren't allowed to take the books home with us, but because I knew the stories so well I could recite them almost word for word to my sisters and brothers when I saw them in the holidays. However many times I reread the stories, I never tired of them.

My dad instilled a love of books into me and all my sisters and brothers from an early age. Other soldiers would go to the mess to drink when they'd finished working, but he would bring home books from the barracks library and read all kinds of enchanting children's stories to us or listen to educational programmes on the radio with us. He really was a very devoted father.

I took off fast with my reading and writing. It was as enjoyable as playing for me. I also soon learned to join in with the tricks and games of the other children. If Mama Salome left her room after she'd cooked herself some tasty food, we sneaked in and licked out her pots. When she returned to wash up, she would see a trail of telltale finger marks around them.

'Who's been licking out my pots?' she would ask, trying to sound cross. None of us ever wanted to own up.

There was a big organisation called Kindernothilfe, based in Europe, that raised some money for the school. The children also had individual sponsors and mine were members of a church in Germany. They sent me a beautiful doll that could blink with its eyelids and eyelashes. Not all of our dolls were so fancy – we used to try to make simple ones out of sticks. We were asked to write thank-you letters to our sponsors and sometimes they took photos of us holding the gifts they had sent us.

Along with our academic subjects, we girls were taught how to bathe properly. Health professionals came to talk to us about good hygiene – keeping our nails short and our hair combed. At first I struggled to comb my hair, but after a while I got to grips with it. My hair was longer than that of some of the other girls and the staff told my parents to cut it short to make it easier to manage.

My dad used to give me a soap called Fa that smelled of wild flowers and sometimes my friends asked me if they could use it. I loved the smell of their soap as well and sometimes got tired of my own. Giggling, we would agree to swap. We enjoyed smelling a little bit different from usual when we showered.

* * *

Although I adapted well to Joyland, I counted the days until I returned home for the first time a few months later. My mum came on the bus to pick me up and as soon as I saw her I flung my arms around her neck.

'Oh, Anne, you've grown a lot,' she said. 'I can see that this place is treating you well. We've all missed you so much.'

On the long bus journey home I chattered all the way about the different things I was doing at Joyland. My mum listened patiently. 'You're certainly different on this journey than on the one when we took you there,' she smiled.

My family were excited when I arrived home. We spent the first few days swapping stories. Excitedly, I told everyone about the running water, showers and flushing toilets at Joyland. They all seemed very impressed.

I had also now seen white people for the first time. I discussed these strange creatures with my sisters. We concluded that they weren't the same kind of humans as us. I believed that they never went to the toilet and could not die.

Although I'd got used to living away from home, I slotted back into family life straight away. I loved the pampering I received at home. My dad slaughtered a chicken in my honour, saying, 'Now I have all my family together.' Chicken was a luxury that wasn't eaten too often in most families.

I taught my siblings the songs I'd learned at school. They were very different from the songs they were learning. I proudly showed off the pens and crayons I had been given at school and received admiring gasps from my brothers and sisters, who didn't possess such luxuries. My school books were also better than my brothers' and sisters' books and I was wearing nice clothes that the Salvation Army had given me.

When the other children in the barracks saw the good things I'd returned home with, they suddenly wanted to be my friend. But their parents forbade them from playing with me. 'Don't touch her or you'll get an infection,' some of them said.

I could never understand why these parents thought that my toys were safe for their children to be in contact with when I wasn't.

Many of my aunts and uncles visited me while I was at home and showered me with love and affection.

'Anne, you're doing so well, you look so strong and healthy,' they exclaimed.

It was hard returning to Joyland after having such a lovely time at home, but I soon settled back into the school routine. I loved being at home but I also loved school, where I felt equal with the others. School also made me aware that some children were less able than me. School and home became my two heavens.

Christmases at the school were very special. A strange-looking man called Father Christmas would give us all a gift with our name on it. I hadn't known anything about these Western traditions before I started at Joyland and felt worried at first because Father Christmas was dressed from head to toe in red. Plain red is associated with lightning in the area where my family's village is, so I was afraid to approach him in case he struck me with lightning. When the staff reassured me, I was brave enough to sit on his knee.

As part of the Christmas celebrations every class had to perform a nativity play. I was always given the part of an angel, but one year I became bored at the thought of doing the same thing again and refused point blank.

'No, I want to be Mary this year,' I said rather petulantly.

'No, you are very good at being an angel. You must be an angel,' my teacher replied.

'But I want to be Mary. Angels don't wear callipers and crutches,' I protested.

The teacher slapped me for my impertinence and I went flying across the room. I wasn't hurt, but I reported it to one of the Salvation Army staff and the teacher was reprimanded. Violence from staff was extremely rare at Joyland.

I had lost a lot of coordination through the polio, but the physiotherapy I received at Joyland helped me to regain some skills. Because I had so much love and positive reinforcement from my family and from the staff at the school, I rarely regarded my disability as a curse, but rather as an inconvenience that I had to work around. Some of the children, though, seemed very miserable about their disability because it had led to their families rejecting them. I always came back to school after the holidays looking immaculate because I had been well looked after, but some of the children came back with scabies because they had been neglected at home. I realised how lucky I was to have a family who loved me.

My years at school were very happy, but by the time I was eight I was more aware that I fitted in at school and at home, but I didn't fit in with the rest of the world. I felt as if the wider community were shouting in my face, 'You are so different, Anne!' because they stared at me wherever I went.

One school holiday when my mum came to pick me up and we got on the bus to go back to Nairobi, the bus conductor said to my mum, 'You have to hold your crippled daughter on your knee and cover her legs so that nobody sees her.'

I burst into tears at his harsh words but, wanting to avoid a fuss, my mum did as she was told.

I was beginning to understand that the world could be very cruel. Whenever we went out in Nairobi during that school holiday I felt that people's eyes were burning through my clothes to stare at my withered polio legs. I was convinced that they dismissed me as an inferior cripple. The stares made me self-conscious and withdrawn in the company of strangers and I longed to return to

Joyland where the staff worked hard to instil confidence and a strong sense of self-belief into us. As soon as I walked back through the school gates I came alive again.

Chapter Four

A Terrible Loss

I t was Saturday 30 June 1979, right in the middle of the rainy season. I was nine years old and had been at Joyland for four years. Saturday was the day we sat outside and styled each other's hair after we had completed our chores. We wore our own clothes at weekends and were all in a happy mood.

The day started like any other. The more able girls weeded the flowerbeds, while the rest of us cleaned our dormitories. Then one of the teachers came in and said abruptly, 'Oh, Anne Olympia, you need to go home.'

I started laughing and said. 'I'm not a fool. It's not closing day yet. I can't go home until the end of term.'

'Yes, you can. Get your things together. You have to go home because your mum wants you. Come with me to the office.'

I had no idea what the teacher was talking about, but we had been taught to obey our teachers, so I did as I was told.

When I got to the office I saw my big sister Alice there.

'Hi, Alice,' I said breezily. I wondered why she had come to my school. It was usually my mum who picked me up at the end of term and brought me back afterwards.

'Where's Mum?' I asked. 'The teacher says she wants me at home.'

I was beginning to feel uneasy. Something wasn't right.

'Oh, she asked me to collect you,' said Alice, trying to sound casual but not quite managing it.

'But where is Mum? And aren't you supposed to be at school?'

'Come, Anne, we need to return home,' she said, without offering any further explanation. 'There's a taxi outside waiting to take us to the bus station.'

She had got a bus from Webuye to Kisumu town and from there had got a taxi to Joyland.

I hurriedly packed some things and anxiously followed Alice into the waiting taxi and then got the bus to my mum's village. My cousins and uncles were gathered at the bus stop with a bicycle to transport me to the centre of the village. I couldn't understand why we were there rather than in Nairobi and why there was such a large group of family members waiting for me.

As I was wheeled along the dusty track local women kept running up to me, wailing and crying, 'Oh, Ruth, you have died and left this flower. Who is going to look after it now?'

What on earth were they talking about? Surely my lovely mum couldn't be dead. The village women must have made a mistake.

I started screaming. 'Where's Mum? Where's Mum?' I cried.

Nobody answered. We arrived at the main part of the village and the terrible truth was confirmed: I could see that my mum was laid out on a bed outside her family's home.

Nothing felt real. My mum had been a strong and healthy woman and she wasn't old. Was I stuck in a horrible dream? I couldn't take in what was going on.

One of my relatives carefully placed me next to my mum. I flung myself on top of her, willing her to start breathing again.

'Mum, Mum, wake up! You promised to make me a jumper, where is it?' I sobbed. I hoped that she would hear me and remember her promise and that would be enough to coax her back to life.

The shock was too much. I told myself that it was all a terrible mistake and that she'd wake up and give me a cuddle very soon. How could she leave me when I needed her so much?

'I'm sorry, Anne,' Alice said, with tears in her eyes. 'We don't know what happened to her, but she really has gone.'

At that time nobody had mobile phones and few Kenyans had landlines, so circulating good or bad tidings always took a long time. It had taken five days for the news of my mum's death to reach my dad, who was working in Nairobi. One of his friends had travelled from the village to the district commissioner and asked him if he could get a message to my dad. The district commissioner had sent a telegram to the Department of Defence in Nairobi and only after that had my dad been informed of his wife's death.

He couldn't believe it. 'She only left Nairobi a few days ago and there was nothing wrong with her then,' he said over and over again.

My mum had been in her village attending a memorial service for her brother, who had recently died, and had collapsed at his graveside and died herself. In those days people were rarely rushed to hospital, nor did they have post-mortems, so the exact cause remained a mystery. As usual when people didn't have a rational explanation they attributed it to witchcraft and said it was the result of a curse, although why my mum had been cursed nobody knew.

People said that her last words as she set off to pay her respects to her brother were that she hoped my youngest brother Geoffrey would be weaned by the time she returned. He was two and a half and she was struggling to get him off the breast. She hadn't expected to be gone for long and hadn't envisaged just how absolute the weaning process would be.

I couldn't think straight. I had never thought that my mum might die. She had always been there for me and I had assumed that she always would be. I felt very lost and empty at the thought of continuing life without her and sobbed uncontrollably.

Alice tried her best to comfort me. 'I promise I will look after you, Anne,' she said, 'just like our mum did.'

I was amazed at how strong she sounded.

A carpenter was enlisted to make a coffin to carry the body from my mum's village to my dad's village, half a day's walk away. It was traditional for a wife to be buried in her husband's village.

I was taken on a bicycle and spent the whole of the bumpy journey crying.

Finally we arrived in my dad's village. I looked around at the place I had been born in but barely remembered. It was the first time I'd been back since we'd been forced out. I remembered the wild roses growing outside our front door. They were still there.

The village was full of people sitting and weeping. My mum had been a very popular figure and everybody was sharing their memories of her. There's much to recommend the African system of mourning. People let their grief spill out freely and don't hold back their emotions. This helps them to heal more quickly.

Nobody paid too much attention to me or asked whether I'd eaten or wanted to wash myself. I thought of how Mum had devoted herself to making sure I had everything I needed. The realisation washed over me in sickly waves that nothing would ever be the same again for me.

My dad was in such deep shock that he could barely comfort us. He looked as if he was in a trance. Although his head had absorbed the news, his heart had not. And he was left with eight children ranging from 16 to two and a half.

I clung onto Alice and during the whole of the mourning period I barely left her side. I took her at her word when she said she would be a replacement mum for me. Whenever she left the room I cried out, 'Where are you going, Alice? Please don't leave me.' I was scared that if I let her out of my sight she would suddenly drop down dead too.

I didn't fully understand the traditional death rituals of our village, but Alice tried to explain them as best she could. My mum's body was placed under a tree facing in a particular direction to symbolise the fact that she had been a married woman. Then everyone gathered around to hear the telling of her life story.

The digging of the grave traditionally begins at midnight. I was exhausted by this time and drifted off to sleep in Alice's arms. Mum's grave was in the homestead, because that was where married women were buried. We didn't have a system of cemeteries and people were generally buried close to where they lived.

At least one cow is slaughtered to mark someone's passing. But first it has to spend the night dancing by the grave. It is hypnotised by people in the village who know how to do such things and then the singing and dancing starts. People sing to send the spirit of the dead person away so that they're not annoyed with the living and come back and haunt them. When the dancing of humans and cow is complete, the cow is slaughtered and then cooked in a stew to be shared by all the mourners. Different parts of it are given to different families.

Funerals sometimes attract hangers-on because it is the duty of the mourners to provide food for those who come to mourn with them. A death means that poor people can not only come and pay their respects but also feed their children for a few days.

On the third day after the funeral we were taken to the river and had our heads shaved.

'They say that your hair dies with your mother and you have to start anew with fresh hair,' Alice explained to me. 'Don't look round,' she urged as we made our way back home. 'They say the spirit of the dead person is there.'

To me, the mourning period seemed to go on forever. Every day new people appeared and they were still coming a month later. They all wailed and threw themselves on my mum's grave.

When the mourning period did finally end, I refused to go back to school. I continued to cling to Alice, who tried her best to hide her own grief and be a surrogate mum to me. I was scared that if I became separated from my family again it would only be a matter of time before another person I loved died. And I didn't want to risk that.

We stayed with my mum's sister in the village. Nobody said anything to my face, but some people muttered that it should have been me who died, not my mum. Others cried for me and worried who would look after a vulnerable girl like me and the younger children. It was a struggle for a family of eight to be without a mother.

I found it very hard being back in the village after the comfort and support of Joyland. I spent most of my time in the bedroom, seeing only close family members. My world had completely crumbled. Here I was back in the environment where people had been scornful of me, and the one person who had always protected me had gone and wasn't going to come back. I felt as if I had died with her.

Pure physical survival was difficult because the village wasn't geared up for people with disabilities. My sisters Jane and Alice brought me water from the river. They tried their best to make me feel better, but they were still young, they too were grieving and it wasn't the same as having my mum around.

I started looking at the world through different eyes. I realised that it was very difficult to survive without maternal support.

There was some discussion among our relatives about who should take in the motherless girls and boys. Only my grandmother wanted me; all the others said I would be a heavy burden. My grandmother really loved me and had often helped my mum to look after me during school holidays. But my dad refused to share his children out. 'The older ones will help the younger ones and I will do the rest,' he said firmly.

I missed more than one school term, but eventually my family managed to persuade me to return. My dad told me repeatedly how important it was for me to continue with my studies.

'You will do your mum proud if you go back,' he coaxed. 'Now your mum has died, I'll try to be both a mum and a dad to you. You must return to school to please both of us.'

Not wanting to do anything that might upset my mum in case she was watching over me, I agreed. My dad took me back on the bus, a journey I had always made with my mum. I was tearful, but my dad urged me to be strong.

The school had regular visiting days when parents could come to see their children.

'Mum always used to come for visiting days. Will you come instead, Dad?'

'I promise you that I'll come and visit you as often as I can, Anne, but sometimes when I'm doing training exercises it will be hard for me to visit,' he said.

I had to be satisfied with that.

* * *

I settled back into the school routine, although I often longed to have my mum back near me.

At first my dad came to visit me often, bringing gifts of army food like corned beef, dried biscuits and sweets, which were big treats for me and the other children in my dormitory. When visiting days came around I would peer out of the gate, anxiously hoping that he would appear. But his visits became less and less frequent.

It was traditional for parents to bring gifts of bananas and bread and for children who received them to share them out with others in the dormitory. One visiting day my dad didn't come but the girl in the bed next to me had received lots of bananas. How my mouth watered for one of them. In the end I couldn't contain myself. I pretended to be sick so that I could stay in the dormitory and stole one of her bananas and some of her bread.

She cried when she saw that one of her juicy bananas was missing and I was accused of stealing it. I squashed the banana peel in my hand, but didn't manage to conceal it very well – I wasn't a very good liar or thief.

'Anne, you must apologise to your friend for stealing from her and you must also apologise to God,' I was told. 'Your punishment will be to sit alone in the dormitory for half an hour.'

I knew I'd done something wrong. I felt so guilty and vowed never to do anything like that again.

Even though my dad had explained to me that he might not always be able to come and see me, I became increasingly distressed when he didn't turn up. I started to doubt him and wondered if he no longer loved me because I was disabled. I wrote him a letter accusing him of not loving me enough.

'I wish Mum had never died,' I wrote. 'This would never have happened when she was alive.' I concluded by saying, 'I didn't write an application to be born.'

My dad wrote me a very long letter back, saying how much he loved me. He also sent a letter to the school, asking them to give me extra care. When he couldn't come to visit me he left money at the school so that they could buy me the things that other parents brought for their children.

The teachers tried their best to be supportive towards me in the months after my mum died. My art teacher, Edward, was especially good. He was particularly well-loved by the pupils and we looked upon him as a father figure, a kind man and a fantastic musician too. He sometimes talked to me about my mum and how her spirit lived on and watched over me even though her body was no longer with us.

'The Lord is watching over you,' he said, 'and so is your mum. You must do well in your studies to do her proud.'

Even though I didn't see the point of some of the things Edward was saying, it made me feel better to know that he was looking out for me. Like my dad, he believed in me and was convinced that I could go on to achieve great things in life.

'Your parents gave you the name Olympia because they believed you were going to achieve great things,' he reminded me. 'You mustn't disappoint them.'

I didn't want to disappoint Edward, but I was hopeless at drawing.

He studied my hands carefully and said, 'Let's try and find what those fingers can do. Everybody has a special talent.'

I longed to be able to draw like a pupil called Noah. He could look at someone's face and translate it into a perfect image on a piece of paper. But however hard I tried, I couldn't draw half as well as he could. I hoped that Edward was right and that some other talent would emerge.

Happily, it already had. I loved singing every night and my voice turned out to be strong and tuneful. I couldn't decipher the words to the James Brown songs my dad had listened to, but I could understand all the words in the a capella tunes on biblical themes we were taught, and I loved singing them.

To my delight, the teachers often chose me to be the lead singer when we entered competitions and performed in different churches. They made sure I looked my best and put coconut oil on my hair to make it shine. Singing gave all of us at Joyland a huge amount of pleasure and always lifted our spirits. Anyone who walked around in the evenings would hear sweet music drifting from every dormitory.

*   *   *

The school decided that because my mum was dead and my dad was often absent it would be better if I was adopted. They contacted a German family who agreed to take me. Little was explained to me and I was too young to fully understand what was going on. But I burst into tears when I overheard one of the house mothers talking to one of the Salvation Army officers about sending me away.

'Does that mean I'll never see my brothers and sisters again?' I asked, sobbing.

They looked startled that they'd been overheard. 'No, no, Anne,' said the house mother. 'Please don't worry, nothing has been decided yet. But if you do move you'll have a better life – and so many toys.'

I wasn't worried about the toys, but the thought of suddenly being transplanted into a family of strangers in a strange land and never seeing my own family again filled me with dread.

At that time my family and school were the only worlds I knew and I didn't want to venture into any others. I became scared to go to sleep in case I woke up in a different place and couldn't find my way back home. I was convinced that I could be snatched under the cover of darkness, and felt a rising sense of panic every time I watched the sun setting. I had received regular gifts from my German sponsors, high-quality books and toys that weren't available in Kenya, and had always looked forward to receiving them, but now I was scared to accept them in case it made it easier for me to be taken away from Joyland.

My dad hadn't visited for a few months and once again I became convinced that he no longer wanted me. I lay down on my bed and sobbed. Things were going from bad to worse. First my mum had died, then my dad hadn't come to visit and now I was being given away. I began to feel permanently frightened.

I started to sit under a big, shady tree where I had a good view of the front gate. I kept my eyes fixed on that gate in the hope that my dad would appear to take me away. But he never did.

After a few months, just when I'd given up hope of ever seeing my dad again, one of the teachers hurried up to me and said, 'Oh, Anne, your dad has arrived.'

Joy surged through me. I hugged and hugged my dad. He swung me round and round and seemed just as pleased to see me as I was to see him.

'Oh, Dad,' I said, 'I thought you were never going to come back, I was sure you didn't love me anymore. I beg you, don't leave me here any longer. Please take me with you. I want to go home right now. They're trying to send me away, but I don't want to go. If they make me leave, I'll never see any of you ever again.'

My words tumbled out so fast they barely made any sense, and tears rolled down my cheeks, but my dad wiped them away with his handkerchief.

'What kind of foolish talk is that, Anne?' he said, stroking my hair. 'I'm your father and I'll always be your father. I'll never abandon you. Please stop worrying.'

Hearing that made me feel very happy. But I was still concerned.

'I must go home with you now, because things can change,' I said.

'Nothing is going to change, I promise you,' Dad said reassuringly. 'You're at Joyland not because we don't love you or care about you but because this is the best place for you to get a good education and learn how to be independent. I don't come more often because I can't get too much time off from the army, that's all.'

We went to the dormitory and my dad spent a long time playing games with me. Having him all to myself was an exquisite luxury.

'Don't worry about anything, Anne,' he said. 'I'm going to speak to the Salvation Army people about your future. I'll make sure that you're not sent away. None of us wants to lose you.'

Once again he left money with the staff to buy me the things that other parents brought their children because he knew that he wouldn't be able to visit me often.

'Just because I can't be here with you as often as some of the other parents doesn't mean that I love you any the less,' he promised me. 'If I don't work hard I won't be able to afford to send all of you children to school, and you know that making sure that all of you get a good education is the most important thing in the world to me.'

I nodded.

'I do understand, Dad.'

But understanding didn't make it any easier for me to cope with his long absences.

A few weeks after my dad's visit to Joyland a pupil called Tom died. We saw him being carried out of the dormitory in his bed with the covers over his face. Many of the children hadn't come across death before and all of us suddenly became scared of simple things like going to the toilet alone.

We mourned Tom. He had been a very quiet seven-year-old boy. Like me, he had walked on callipers and crutches. I never knew exactly what was wrong with him and we never discovered why he had died.

'Don't cry,' said one of the house mothers soothingly. 'Tom is at peace now. He's in heaven and has become one of the stars. You can see him if you gaze at the sky at night.'

Nobody had mentioned anything about stars to me when my mum died. I found it comforting to think that she had become a star too. That night I looked up at the inky black sky, focused on the brightest star and hoped that it was her.

Chapter Five

The Coup

I developed a reputation as a real tomboy. Despite the constraints of my paralysed legs, my callipers and my crutches, I loved to climb and to take risks. There were a few bunk beds at Joyland for the more able-bodied children and even though it was way beyond the capacity of a girl with my disability, I sometimes tried to haul myself onto the top bunk using my upper body strength. Sometimes I got stuck, but it didn't stop me from persevering.

We were expected to wash our hands thoroughly before we went to the dining hall. One day for a joke I decided that I was going to wash my legs too. I went to the sink and removed my callipers. My friend lifted one of my legs up to wash it. I was holding the tap with wet hands and I slipped and fell. Instantly I screamed in agony. I had never felt such severe pain in my life. My leg was trapped under the sink.

There were some builders outside. They rushed over and tried to pull my leg out. My whole body was on fire with pain.

'Please don't let me die!' I cried.

The school nurse put me in a wheelchair and took me in a taxi to Kisumu General Hospital, about half an hour away. The first thing they did was to give me some pain-killers, followed by an X-ray, which revealed that my right hip was broken. They put me in plaster, bringing back memories of the time when I was encased in plaster after my polio was first diagnosed. My leg was suspended in mid-air in traction with weights attached to it.

Although the doctors admitted me, they weren't sure what to do with me. They didn't know whether my hip was twisted from polio or from the fall. So they referred me to a more sophisticated hospital, Russia Hospital, and I was put on an adult orthopaedic ward there.

I was furious with myself for being stupid enough to try and put my leg in the sink. Although it hadn't been easy getting around on callipers and crutches, at least I had been mobile. Now I was completely stuck.

At first I loathed being in hospital. The food was bad and I was sometimes left sitting on a bedpan for a long time. But I cheered up twice a week when my friends came to visit me. We played games together and they brought me sweets and filled me in on all the Joyland news. When I became mobile enough to drag myself around, I found the children's wards and started playing with the other children. The teachers at Joyland also sent work to the hospital for me to do so that I didn't fall too far behind with my studies.

The school felt very responsible for what had happened, even though it wasn't their fault. The staff visited me regularly, pampered me and brought me special drinks and sweets.

My friends were good too. Sarah was once given an orange for her supper as a special treat. Instead of eating it all herself, she saved half of it for me, a gesture which really touched me.

She was a mischievous girl who had once stolen a cigarette from the workmen and encouraged me to try it. I had almost choked to death when I tried to inhale. The staff were furious and said the fire on a cigarette was like the fire that burned in hell. 'If you smoke, you're heading to hell,' they told me. I was terrified and never touched a cigarette again.

In hospital I lay back and made the most of all the treats and attention that came my way. The staff treated me very well, at least partly because I was connected to white people. It was four months before I was finally discharged and my hip has never fully healed. To this day it is more twisted than my left and makes a clicking sound.

I had enjoyed being the centre of attention in hospital but I had missed school life and my friends and was delighted that my life was getting back to normal.

A few months after I returned to school the teachers told me I had been selected to be head girl for the year. We were all expecting another girl to be chosen, who was very loud and confident, and when I found out they had chosen me instead I laughed. I had never considered myself head girl material.

'Why do you think they chose me?' I asked Mama Salome.

'Well, you have matured a lot, Anne,' she said, 'because of the various problems you've had, losing your mother and breaking your hip. We all think you'll do a good job. You don't get involved in arguments, you look out for others and want to make sure they're happy. You're good at playing the peacemaker.'

Once it had sunk in that they were being serious about wanting me for head girl, I was overjoyed. I felt very proud.

Becoming head girl made me look at myself differently. For the first time I started focusing on what I could do rather than what I couldn't. Before I had considered myself lacking in so many ways. For a start, I was one of the thinnest in the school and I was worried that some of the students wouldn't respect me because I was so skinny. In Africa people have more status if they're fatter because it's considered a sign of greater wealth. Thinness is associated with poverty. But being thin didn't seem to cause me any problems in my new role.

My parents had instilled it in me that everyone should be treated the same because we were all equal. I tried to apply these rules and the pupils did seem to respect me.

My main role was to act as peacekeeper and make sure there was no bullying going on. I made sure that all the children were included. I also encouraged the older children to look after the younger ones.

If there was any misconduct from the students I was expected to tell a house mother. Sometimes one of them would come and say, 'Is there a problem?' I tried to get the balance right between protecting pupils from the wrath of the teachers and acting responsibly and reporting behaviour that was of real concern. I didn't like 'grassing up' children who had misbehaved and only spoke to the teachers if something very serious occurred.

Back in Nairobi my dad had married a woman called Florence. He asked us to call her 'Mum', which none of us was happy about at first because she wasn't our mum. But because she was so kind and nice and looked after all of us so well, we soon grew to love her, although she could never be a replacement for my beloved mum. My dad had moved into a bigger apartment, which was much more comfortable, and my step-mum made a nice home for the family there. I always looked forward to going home and seeing everybody.

In August 1982, shortly after my dad's marriage, we heard rumours that the government had been overthrown in a military coup. I didn't understand much about politics, but started to worry about my dad.

'Could he be one of those trying to get rid of our government?' I said to one of my friends.

It was almost the end of term, but parents were asked to collect their children a few days earlier than usual because nobody knew what was going to happen next. My dad gave instructions for me to be put on the overnight bus to Nairobi.

I burst into tears at the prospect of travelling alone on the bus, something I had never done before.

'You'll be fine,' said Mama Salome. 'You're a big girl now and your dad will meet you at the other end.'

A Salvation Army major put me on the bus, explained about my disability to a group of laughing, chattering women carrying big boxes of freshly fried fish, and asked them to look after me. They were taking the fish from Lake Victoria to Nairobi to sell. They were kind, looked after me well and carried me out of the bus whenever we had toilet stops.

Our journey was slowed down by many police checks. Every time the police gestured for the bus to stop I peered out of the window anxiously, wondering if we'd ever make it to Nairobi.

All the talk was about the political situation.

'It's the air force who are fighting the army,' said one passenger.

'The army is staying loyal to the government,' said another.

Some passengers said it wasn't safe to travel to
Nairobi at all, but the driver dismissed their concerns. 'If
I don't get this bus to Nairobi I'm going to get the sack,'
he said firmly. 'Have faith. I'll do my best to get you all
there safely.'

We did finally reach the city and it was as we pulled
into the bus station that the soldiers boarded the bus
and my dad appeared at just the right moment to rescue
me.

I was so relieved to see him, but even he couldn't
shield me from the horror of the coup. As we raced
through the streets I saw injured people staggering and
moaning. Never in my life had I witnessed such scenes. I
was horrified, and felt bewildered and lost. The world
seemed to be spiralling out of control.

When we reached a clock tower in the centre of
Nairobi, my dad unlocked the door and bundled me
inside.

'Don't cry, Anne, it will all be over soon,' he said. 'Stay
here quietly and I promise I'll be back as soon as I can to
collect you. Don't make a sound and you'll be safe.'

He hurried out and locked the door behind him.

There was hardly any space inside the tower. I stood
there in my callipers and crutches, not knowing what to
do. I was absolutely terrified at being locked in this
cramped, dark, musty space.

'What if something happens to my dad?' I thought.
'Nobody will know I'm hiding in here and I'll starve to
death.'

My hands started to go numb as they clutched my crutches. I cried, I wet myself and eventually I found a way to sit down.

Finally I dozed off, only to be woken by screams and gunshots. It was the first time I had ever heard guns being fired and I couldn't believe what a horribly loud noise they made. Then things went quiet again.

After a while I could hear feet pounding by so loudly and heavily that I thought the clock tower must be surrounded by a herd of stampeding elephants.

Voices were calling out, 'Oh, help me, help me, I'm dying!' and 'I can't leave my child and run!'

I had no way of knowing what was happening.

Gradually the footsteps faded away and I nodded off again.

When I woke, it seemed as though I'd been in the clock tower for an eternity. I tried to work out what was going on from the sounds coming from outside, but it was impossible to guess.

Eventually I heard the sound of a key turning in the lock.

'Dad! Dad!' I cried out hoarsely.

My dad stood there drenched in sweat and looking agitated. 'Come, Mamy, I'm going to take you home now,' he said.

I was flooded with relief. I had been in the clock tower for 12 hours.

As my dad carried me out, I could see dead bodies lying in the street and hear gunfire all around. I was terrified that we were going to be hit. The air was filled with acrid smoke. I had watched plenty of Chuck Norris movies without batting an eyelid, but this was completely different. I wished that all the soldiers and bodies could disappear into a TV screen so that normal life could resume.

Once we got safely back to the barracks my dad sank down into a chair. He looked completely exhausted. He introduced me to Florence for the first time and she and my sisters helped me to wash myself and change my clothes.

'Dad, please can you explain to me what's going on?' I asked, when we'd both recovered a bit. 'It feels like the world is going to end.'

My dad smiled wearily. 'I don't think you need worry about that just yet, Anne. This business will all be finished with soon. A group of soldiers from the air force, led by Hezekiah Ochuka, took over the Voice of Kenya radio station and announced that they had overthrown the government. Most of the army was out on exercise in the bush at the time, so the government's defences were low. But the army has stayed loyal to the government and we have managed to suppress the coup. Things will return to normal very soon.'

My dad was right. For the first two days after the coup there was a 24-hour curfew, and after that a 12-hour curfew, but within a few days it was as if the attempted coup had never happened. The government announced that 145 people had been killed, though, and my dad told me that others had behaved very badly, looting televisions and fridges from the wealthy, not realising they couldn't use them in the slums where there was no electricity.

When my dad explained his role in stopping the coup I felt extremely proud of him. 'You're my hero,' I said. Now I could understand why he was too busy to come and see me often. It completely changed the way I looked at him. I could see how devoted he was to his country and thought, 'If he loves his country so much he must love me even more.'

Although order was restored quickly, the coup left us all feeling very nervous. People no longer trusted the government and doubted the stability of everything in Kenya. Whenever aeroplanes flew over we were terrified that they were going to drop a bomb on us.

I suffered terrible nightmares as a result of being locked in the clock tower and sometimes woke up sweating and screaming. I became very scared of crowds and loud noises. Had I been in the West I would probably have been given trauma counselling.

I told my dad about it.

'You'll feel better soon,' he promised.

The family prayed for me at church and sure enough after a few months the trauma did start to fade.

For years afterwards, though, I was frightened of travelling in and out of the bus station in Nairobi. There I relived all the terrible things I had seen and heard on the day of the coup.

Chapter Six

Growing Up

During the school holidays when I was in the barracks in Nairobi, I had a stomach ache one day and then discovered lots of blood in my underwear.

I screamed out, 'Help me, help me, I'm dying!'

Esther, a friend who lived in the barracks, rushed up to me. 'What on earth is the matter, Anne?'

'I think my intestines are coming out. I'm going to die!' I cried. 'There's blood everywhere!'

Esther started to explain. 'You're not going to die – you've started your periods, that's all. It's a sign that you're a normal woman.'

I didn't know what she was talking about and wasn't convinced that everything was alright.

'Shouldn't I be going to hospital?' I asked.

'No,' she laughed. 'You'll be fine.'

She tried to explain to me how babies were made. It was something my mum and older sisters had never discussed with me, so I was completely in the dark about the way women's bodies worked. I wasn't sure that I liked the sound of becoming a woman and certainly didn't want to be bothered with bleeding every month. I wanted to remain an innocent child. But whether I liked it or not, I was growing up.

This also meant my time at Joyland was drawing to a close and I had to make the transition to secondary school.

Which secondary school students attended was determined by how well they did in their exams. Everybody across Kenya did the same entrance exam – a tough test in maths, English and science called the Kenya Certificate of Primary Education.

I was absolutely thrilled when I found out I'd done well enough to get into Kereri Girls' School. The teachers at Joyland had encouraged me to choose this school because it had a strong academic reputation. It offered good A-level courses and a high percentage of its students went on to university.

My dad was very proud of me. 'I knew you could do it, Anne Olympia. I'm sure you'll go far in life,' he said with tears in his eyes.

As the date when I was due to start school loomed closer, however, I became more and more apprehensive. Everything had been so safe and secure at Joyland. I had been surrounded by caring staff and by children who faced similar challenges to me. How would I cope in a mainstream school where most people had never met anyone who dragged themselves along on callipers and crutches and where the facilities would be geared towards able-bodied students? I began to question whether secondary school was a good idea or not.

'Maybe I should just try to learn a skill like being a cobbler instead,' I said to my dad.

'Don't be silly, Anne,' he replied. 'You'll be just as good a student as the rest of them, and probably better. It's very important that you continue with your education.'

He took me to school on the bus on my first day.

'Don't be so anxious, you'll be fine,' he said, seeing my scared expression.

When we arrived at the school there were people milling around everywhere. It seemed as if everybody but me knew what to do and where to go.

It was the rainy season and the earth beneath my feet had turned to mud. My crutches slid around and I lost control of them and fell flat on my face. My hands, face and previously pristine school uniform were all coated in red, sticky mud. Even though I didn't want to look like a cry-baby on my first day, I couldn't stop myself from sobbing. I wanted to die of embarrassment. I was sure that all the other girls were whispering. 'Oh, look at that girl with metal all over her legs, walking with metal sticks. She can't even get around. And now she's all dirty. What on earth is she doing here?'

My dad helped me up and tried to clean the worst of the mud off me. 'Anne, stop crying and be strong. You

can overcome this,' he said. I'm sure his heart was breaking to see his daughter struggling so much.

'I *can't* overcome it, Dad. Please take me home with
you. This has all been a big mistake. How am I going to
manage to get around this school? It's not like Joyland,
specially built for people like me. Please, please take me
home with you, Dad. It will be humiliating for me to stay
at this place.'

My dad knew how difficult things were going to be for
me, but he didn't want to damage my shaky confidence
even further, so he said, 'What kind of talk is that, Anne?
I'm sure the other girls and the teachers will help you
with the things you can't manage to do by yourself. I have
to go now, but I'll come and visit you as soon as I can.'

I hugged him, inhaling his fresh, clean smell. I didn't
want to let him go. More tears rolled down my cheeks as
I watched him walk away.

The prefects and teacher on duty showed the new
arrivals the way to the dormitory and after that we were
left to find our own way, to sink or swim.

'Welcome to the real world, Anne,' I said to myself.
'This is how life is. Don't expect the kind of soft treatment you got at Joyland. Somehow you're going to have
to find a way to survive here.'

I discovered later that new girls had the nickname
'Mono', although I never discovered why.

There was a step going down to my dormitory and I
wasn't used to such things. I fell on my elbow, bruising
it badly, but was too ashamed to tell anyone that I'd

fallen again. I tried to hide my injury by putting on a cardigan and sank down onto my bed in complete despair. I knew my dad was right and that I needed to give this new place a chance, but the only thing I wanted to do at that moment was run away and never come back. I lay back on my bed and closed my eyes.

Kereri had once been a well-maintained missionary school. The building was sturdy and flushing toilets and showers had been installed. By the time I arrived, however, it had fallen into disrepair. The toilets and showers no longer worked because the water supply had not been maintained. Because there was no longer running water, the girls fetched buckets of water and stored them under their bunk beds. It was impossible for me to do this and I realised I would have to rely on others to do it for me.

The only toilets were pit latrines and because I couldn't squat, I had to sit on the filthy ground. The baths were not accessible to me either, so I had to sit on a stone to bathe myself. I longed to be back at Joyland where everything was clean and easy.

Even meals were difficult. We had to queue for our food, but I just couldn't manage it. The headmistress was sympathetic and arranged for food to be brought to my dormitory. This at least made life a little bit easier.

I didn't get much sleep that first night, partly because my elbow was hurting me so much and partly because I couldn't stop crying at the thought of all the years that stretched ahead of me at Kereri.

The following day my elbow was so swollen that it was difficult to conceal the injury. Eventually it got so badly infected that it was too painful for me to use my crutches and callipers. I could no longer get around and was stuck in the dormitory.

I decided I would have to tell the school nurse about it.

'You silly girl,' she said when she saw my swollen elbow. 'Why didn't you tell us before?'

She cleaned it up and put a dressing on it which she changed twice a day and eventually it healed.

There had been very few students with disabilities at the school and people kept staring, curious to know how I managed. This was one of the hardest things for me. Because most of my life until then had been spent either at home or at Joyland, I wasn't used to it and it made me feel very uncomfortable.

To make matters worse, the other girls seemed afraid to sit close to me. Nobody was cruel to my face, but I heard them whispering to each other, 'Look how thin and misshapen her legs are. How does she sleep? How does she go to the toilet? If I was in her situation I would commit suicide or ask my parents to kill me.'

I was horrified, as taking my life had never crossed my mind. Life had always presented challenges for me, but until now I had felt that I was a loved and valued member of the community. Most of the time I had been very happy. I wondered what these girls would they say if they saw some of the children I had been to school with at Joyland – children who could not speak or turn over when they lay down or feed themselves. But all the pupils there were like brothers and sisters and helped each other. We were encouraged to feel part of a group and to take part in as many activities as possible. I longed to be back there.

For many months things were bleak for me at Kereri. I had problems with my bowels because of my disability, and as a result of having to sit on the dirty ground to use the pit latrine, I was constantly getting infections.

Even the girls who tried to be helpful to me sometimes ended up making me feel worse than ever. One girl walked alongside me one day when I was struggling on my callipers and crutches, screwing up her face to empathise with my pain. I didn't want to be reminded of my disability in this way. I was just living my life the only way I knew how, and was trying to take each day as it came.

Some of the girls looked down on me because of my disability, forgetting that I had scored more highly than some of them in the exam to get a place at the school.

The first time my spirits lifted was when we were sitting in the classroom a few months after I had arrived at Kereri and one of the girls asked the teacher to help her get the right answer to a question.

The teacher replied, 'Go and ask Anne how she got her answer. She understands this topic very well and is one of our brightest students.'

Those kind words made me feel as if I was being bathed in a golden light. I was so grateful to the teacher for showing the other girls that I was more than just 'that crippled girl on callipers and crutches'. I wanted to throw my arms around her neck and say, 'Thank you, thank you, you don't know how much difference this makes to me.' But it wasn't the kind of thing students did to their teachers.

In Kenya parents sacrifice a lot to pay school fees for their children, so the children work hard and value their education. Discipline is much stricter than it is in English schools and the cane is used as a punishment for those who misbehave or are disobedient. 'Spare the rod, spoil the child' is a philosophy that has fallen out of fashion in the West, but in Kenya this was how values were inculcated and discipline enforced when I was at school. Sometimes caning was even carried out in front of the whole school as an extra deterrent to wrongdoers.

In the first months even walking from the dormitory to the classroom was a nightmare for me. In the mornings we were expected to go to the dining room to collect our breakfast porridge then go to assembly before going to our classroom. It was impossible for me to make that journey in the same amount of time as the other girls and so I was allowed to miss assembly, which gave me time to get from breakfast to the classroom before the first lesson started. As I struggled along the corridor I would hear the girls singing beautiful hymns in the morning assembly.

'One day I'd like to stand in the chapel with them and join in the singing,' I thought to myself.

Then one time my crutch broke and I had to wait a few days for it to be welded back together. I was completely stranded without it and had to stay in the dormitory and rely on the other girls to bring me food and water. I was a very independent person and hated not being able to do things for myself.

Gradually, however, I learned ways of coping with school life and stopped being embarrassed about being disabled. I fell often, but instead of bursting into tears as I had done on my first day I giggled, 'Oh, I've fallen flat like a fish,' and the other girls started laughing with me. After that most of them laughed with me rather than at me. Humour can break down barriers and melt prejudices.

Slowly, I began to make friends. I also began to understand that it is normal human behaviour to be curious about someone who looks or behaves differently from you, but it isn't necessarily unkind.

'Will you remove your callipers so we can look at your legs?' asked one friend.

When I did so, the girls could see that one of my feet looked to the right and one looked to the left instead of facing straight ahead. But once they understood exactly what my problems were, they stopped thinking about them.

My friends even took it in turns to carry me back to the dormitory. I would take off my callipers first and someone would carry them and my crutches. We laughed about it and the whole thing became fun instead of a chore.

Having a group of girls who did so much to make my life easier without making any sort of fuss about it lifted my spirits enormously and my heart filled with joy when I realised I was no longer 'Anne with the funny legs and callipers and crutches' to my friends but just 'Anne'. When you have a disability, knowing that you are not defined by it is the sweetest feeling.

Once I knew I had been accepted, I became much more relaxed. My friends also became very protective of me and started inviting me to have pictures taken with them. I often went and sat with them when their parents brought food for them.

One of my friends was a girl called Rhoda, who eventually became head girl. She was softly spoken and very intelligent, and taught me a lot about humility. Although she had many talents and great beauty, she was always modest. We all gravitated towards her. She was a natural leader and became like a mother to us. I felt so comfortable with her. She came from a very strong, dependable background and had been brought up with very good values. I admired everything about her.

Winifred was the friend I sat next to in class. She wore her hair short and had beautiful handwriting. She was always laughing and making jokes. She became a dormitory prefect.

I also had a friend called Evelyn. She was a mischievous girl who was involved in everything at school – drama,
hockey and debating. She was always full of fun and
really made us laugh.

At school we thought we were more sophisticated
than the village girls because we tried to dress in the
way we had seen women on Western television
programmes dress. Sometimes we could be very critical
of people we decided were unfashionable, like our maths
teacher.

'Oh, look, there's the teacher who doesn't know how
to dress properly,' someone would say.

'Oh yes, two people could fit into those baggy clothes.
It's only that ugly belt she's wearing that is keeping
those clothes on her,' I would comment.

'Doesn't she ever look in the mirror before she leaves
the house?' Evelyn would laugh.

While we were happy to criticise unfashionable teachers, what we didn't realise was that some of the television
programmes that were brought in from North and South
America were ten years old, so our attempts at being
fashionable were a decade out of date. If Western teen-
agers had seen them, they would have poked fun at us.

Because I loved fashion so much it really used to
bother me that I couldn't wear high heels and short
skirts. With my misshapen legs of different lengths I
would have looked ridiculous in such clothes. The clothes
I could wear got torn quickly because they were forever
getting snagged on my callipers and crutches. I longed

to look different and feel different. What I really wanted was for the world around me to fit me, but during my teenage years it never did.

Nevertheless, after a few months, when my teachers told me that I was among the top five in the class academically, I felt very proud. I longed to tell my dad. I decided that Kereri wasn't a bad school after all.

I read in the local newspaper that they were running a poetry competition. I decided to enter a poem about accepting the life you have and the importance of going to school and getting a good education. To my amazement, I won.

I loved the buzz of winning. This was even more satisfying than the time the teacher had asked the girl in my class to approach me for help. I felt I had some value as a human being and could achieve things just like anybody else. I began to understand that although I would never be able to compete with the other girls in things like running and jumping, I could certainly compete as an equal intellectually.

The poetry prize was 500 Kenyan shillings, which was about five pounds. It seemed like an enormous sum of money to me and was used to buy library books. I went round beaming from ear to ear because I was so excited. After that the teachers often asked me to recite poems I'd written, which made me feel very proud.

Like my parents, I was a devout Christian, and I joined the school's Christian Union choir. We sang gospel music together and I adored it. The music somehow lifted me out of my body to a happier place where the state of your limbs was irrelevant and only the beauty of the melodies mattered.

Because the facilities and care at the school were not tailored to the needs of disabled people, I still had a few health problems, though. I developed sores on my bottom from sitting on the dirty ground to use the toilet, my hands became infected from crawling on the ground around the toilet and I developed very painful boils caused by pressure from the straps of my callipers.

In the school holidays my step-mum cleaned my callipers with Dettol and helped me give myself a thorough bath and hair wash. She treated me as lovingly as her own daughter and I felt myself becoming much closer to her.

I told my dad about my health problems and he took me to the army dispensary. I was given disposable gloves and a special disinfectant cream to use, as well as some padding for my callipers. When I went back to school I looked so much better because I had been properly looked after at home. I learned to wake up very early and prepare my things for the day and then I used the toilet when all the other girls were in assembly.

Sometimes I had to go to hospital to have my calliper boils treated. Evelyn would accompany me and would go and buy fish and chips for us. These were a welcome change from the maize and beans we ate at school. We always tried to make them last as long as possible so that we would get back to school too late for the afternoon lessons. When it came to my hospital visits, Evelyn and I were partners in crime.

Some of the girls started to help me to wash my clothes because they could see how much I struggled to do it alone. I felt that kindness and cooperation were two of my favourite qualities. I was lucky to be experiencing both.

Sometimes people who didn't know me well would say, 'Oh, you have a beautiful smile' or 'You have a good singing voice' and touch my head or my cheek while standing above me. They meant well, but I couldn't help feeling patronised by such behaviour. My friends became experts at defending me from that sort of attitude. And at the beginning of each new school year, when the latest arrivals were staring at me, they would warn them sternly, 'Don't stare or she'll hit you with her crutch.'

In the school holidays I sometimes returned to Joyland, because they ran a support group for former pupils. My heart always leaped as I arrived at the school gates. For a few days life would be much easier. To be able to have a shower and use clean toilets was wonderful. It restored my dignity. And it was so nice not to have people endlessly asking questions like 'Why is your leg like this?'

The first time I went back to Joyland I had braided extensions into my hair. This was the latest fashion in Kenya and one that my friends at Kereri and I had experimented with. My disabled friends had never seen anything like it. I joked with them that after my mum had died my dad had married a white lady with long black hair and she had cut it off and given it to me. They gasped and seemed to believe me. I really enjoyed playing the joker and didn't tell them the truth about my extensions until just before it was time for us all to leave.

We also shared our problems and talked about how we were faring in the 'able-bodied' world. The staff at Joyland listened attentively to our tales of woe.

'You have to start a secondary school,' I said. 'It's too hard for us to attend normal school. We would find it much easier to continue with our education at a school like this.'

'We just don't have the space to do that,' the staff said.

All of us in the support group did our best to encourage each other to persevere in often difficult circumstances. I realised just how lucky I was to have settled at secondary school. Some had tried it but found it too much of a struggle, dropped out and turned to begging instead.

I was told sad news about Grace, one of my friends from Joyland who was also disabled as a result of polio. She had got pregnant at the age of 15 after a man had taken advantage of her, and had died in childbirth because she hadn't known that a woman with her disability could not have a normal delivery. People in her village had eventually got her to hospital, but it had been too late to save her life.

I was upset to hear this, and terrified as well. I dreamed of having children of my own, but hearing what had happened to Grace made me afraid that if I ever got pregnant the same thing would happen to me. The teachers at Joyland had always warned us never to sit too close to boys or we would get into terrible trouble. At the time I hadn't understood what they meant, but now I began to realise.

Despite this, I left Joyland feeling much more confident. The love and support I had received from the staff and the other returning pupils made me feel much better about myself.

When I wasn't at Joyland I spent school holidays in my dad's barracks in Nairobi. I loved going home and seeing my family again. Florence always did her best to pamper me the way my mum had done. I really loved her now and could see that my sisters and brothers felt the same way.

During one school holiday my friend Abigail from Joyland came to stay in the barracks. I hadn't mentioned to my sisters and brothers that she had an artificial leg. When she took it off to go to sleep, the younger ones all started screaming. The next day they told their friends and lots of children started following her around. They decided that she was some sort of magic person who was not quite human.

*   *   *

Back at school, when the other girls did hockey and other sports, there was nothing for me to do but sit on the field and watch them run around. I was determined not to mope, though, and looked around for something else to do. Eventually I discovered an old out-of-tune piano in the school chapel and every time the other girls had a games lesson I went there and banged the keys aimlessly.

A missionary teacher from Canada called Miss McAllister found me there one day.

'What a terrible racket you're making, Anne. Would you like to learn how to play properly?'

'Yes, I'd love to,' I replied. I always jumped at the chance to learn a new skill.

She started teaching me twice a week, at first guiding my fingers across the keys with her own hands. I soon got a feel for what I was supposed to be doing and started making sounds that resembled basic tunes. I felt very proud of myself and remembered Edward, the art teacher at Joyland who had said I needed to find something that my fingers could do.

Sadly Miss McAllister was diagnosed with stomach cancer and returned to Canada. I really missed her and thought often of how much she had taught me. It made me understand that one of the most important things one human being can do for another is teach them a new skill.

A few months later the headmistress announced that Miss McAllister had died and the whole school broke down and sobbed. She had been a very popular teacher and we all thought she seemed too young to die, especially for a white person.

I carried on bashing away at the piano without her and eventually I started playing by ear. Even though I wasn't very good, one of the teachers asked me to play the piano for the school. At first I played badly, but gradually I improved. I got a few of my friends together and we started a singing group called the Soul Winners, performing gospel music. The music was like therapy for me, giving me the inner strength to cope with the difficult parts of school. I was particularly pleased to find my good singing voice and ability to write lyrics earned me respect from the other girls.

Other people seemed to like what we did too and we started getting invitations to perform at local churches and Christian rallies. The headmistress gave us her blessing and even let us use the school driver and provided a teacher who acted as chaperone. Many girls were envious of us because of these outings from school. We fantasised about being the western Kenyan equivalent of Diana Ross and the Supremes.

During our performances I stood for some of the time on my callipers and crutches, held and supported by my friends. The rest of the time I sat down.

When a teacher died suddenly, spontaneously I gathered some of the girls together and we sang and played the piano as an impromptu memorial. We sang 'Oh God, My Saviour, How Great Thou Art' and 'Rock of Ages,

Cleft to Me,' and 'This Is My Story, This Is My Song', a particularly beautiful hymn. The whole school joined in, mourning the teacher and paying tribute to him. I wished I had known how to sing and play the piano like that when my mum died. I would have loved to have paid tribute to her in that way.

Singing made us all feel better. It lifted our souls and connected body, mind and spirit. One time there was an inter-dormitory singing competition and our dormitory won. I was overjoyed to be part of the winning team.

The more settled I became, the better I performed in all areas of school life. The teachers praised me and used me as an example to the other girls. If they were having problems, the teachers said, 'Speak to Anne and find out what drives her forward.'

Sports day was one of the few times that I felt inadequate. I couldn't help being envious of the girls who sprinted effortlessly across the field. I tried to imagine what it would feel like to have hips and legs that worked perfectly, the way God had designed them, and to have them carrying my body fast across the earth.

The winners on sports day had a goat slaughtered in their honour. I felt guilty to be sharing in the feast because I had achieved nothing.

As we sat munching the delicious stewed goat I confided to one of my friends that I longed to be able to do what she could do.

'But you have many other talents, Anne,' she said. 'I can't sing and play the piano the way you can and I never get your grades in tests.' She looked at me thoughtfully for a minute and then asked, 'What happens when you sleep? Are you still wearing your callipers in your dreams?'

I had never really thought about it. I reflected for a moment and then realised that neither my callipers and crutches nor my paralysed legs ever featured in my dreams.

'No,' I replied. 'I'm never disabled in my dreams. I am physically perfect, the way I was when I was born. In my dreams I dance.'

Chapter Seven

Romance

I did well in most of my subjects at Kereri, although my grades were weaker in those where I had to move around. I struggled with getting up and down the few steps to the science laboratory and couldn't join in with the map-reading exercises in geography, which involved walking around the school field.

One of my favourite subjects was poetry. We studied African poetry as well as verse from other continents. One of my favourites was a very funny play called *The Burdens* by John Ruganda. We also studied English literature and I particularly loved Charles Dickens' *Oliver Twist*. I felt so sorry for Oliver because he was poor. I found it hard to imagine that England, which we considered to be a land of plenty, could ever have had such poverty.

My friends and I also discovered trashy English romantic novels and smuggled them into the dormitory to read. Whenever our teachers found them, they confiscated them. The headmistress used to check in girls' suitcases for these books and remove them on the spot. I used to hide them under my mattress or inside my pillow, places the teachers rarely searched. There was a boys' high school next door and we often exchanged forbidden books over the fence.

James Hadley Chase and Barbara Cartland were our favourite authors. It was easier to get hold of their books than classic African literature like Chinua Achebe's works. After reading a handful of Barbara Cartland's books I thought that everyone in England lived a life like her characters. I enjoyed reading about how the hero and heroine fell in love with each other, but was shocked by how the women let the men touch them after they'd only met a couple of times. I liked the way they always lived happily ever after, but wondered if I would ever find that kind of perfect love because of my far from perfect body.

In fact when I read about the beautiful female characters, I couldn't help wondering how someone would write about me. How could the flowery language be adapted to describe my callipers and crutches? I decided that it would take a literary genius to make my body sound appealing in a romantic book.

Although I was aware of falling short of the Mills & Boon ideals, I assumed that the destiny of all white people was to fall madly in love and live happily ever after, even the missionaries we saw in Kenya.

At Joyland they had sometimes showed us religious films and in these films Jesus was always a blue-eyed, blond-haired man, so we associated that colouring with everything good. It was a long time before I realised that those were only pictures, not an accurate portrayal of how Jesus actually looked.

As I matured and met more white people, I did, however, revise my previous view that they never went to the toilet and could not die. Miss McAllister had died, for a start. Eventually I realised they were just like us.

As well as our Mills & Boon contraband we started reading banned magazines like *Viva*, *True Love* and *Drum* – Kenyan magazines full of gossip about love and tips on how to look beautiful and keep your man happy. Whenever we managed to get hold of them we passed them around far and wide.

We didn't have access to make-up, but were very influenced by pictures of models in the magazines looking stunning with bright red lips and extra long eyelashes. We discovered that we could moisten red crepe paper and rub the dye onto our lips and cheeks. At Christmas all the red paper disappeared because we had taken it. We probably looked like clowns, but in our impressionable teenage states decided that we all looked stunningly beautiful.

There was a lot of talk among my friends about boyfriends. Like any other teenage girl I longed to have a boyfriend, but I panicked when I thought about getting too close to a boy in case I ended up like Grace.

There were a few opportunities for the boys from the school next door to meet the girls at our school. Sometimes debates were held or joint Sunday services. Both sexes certainly made the most of these opportunities and all my friends found themselves boyfriends.

I was so well settled at school by this time that I rarely thought about my disability, but now the ugly discrimination I had sometimes experienced reared its head again. None of the boys approached me and I overheard one of them saying to his friend, 'Anne's got a beautiful face. Can you imagine how cool she'd be if she had proper legs? If only she wasn't a cripple.'

When I heard this I fled to the dormitory and sobbed. Why was I fooling myself that I was equal to the other girls? I wasn't the same as them and I never would be.

After a few minutes of crying I washed my face, looked at myself in the mirror and said sternly, 'Anne Olympia, stop all this foolishness. That boy was being thoughtless. One day you will find the perfect man.'

Eventually I did get asked on a date by one boy – it was a disabled boy I'd been at Joyland with. I sensed that he'd asked lots of able-bodied girls to be his girlfriend and that they'd turned him down, so he was approaching me as a last resort.

'No, thank you,' I replied firmly.

I was determined not to be anybody's last resort.

The teachers knew exactly what some of the girls were getting up to with their boyfriends. They came and checked to see whether they were pregnant by squeezing their stomachs. They didn't bother checking mine, though, because they assumed I would never have sex. Being excluded from the stomach squeezing humiliated me. I wanted to feel like the other girls.

'What did they do to you?' I asked my friends when they came back from these tests. They explained that they were asked to partially undress so they could be examined.

'I wish I could have that test,' I said.

If the teachers found any telltale swelling, the girl would be sent to the hospital for a test. If she was found to be pregnant she was sent home in disgrace, but I imagined how overjoyed I would feel if I got pregnant. It would give me a chance to prove that I was as capable of childbearing as the next girl. If I had been thrown out of school for getting pregnant, I would have left with my head held high. There was nothing I wanted as much as to become a mother.

Once I asked the teacher if I could be checked with the other girls.

'Oh, Anne, you don't need it,' she said, understanding how I was feeling. 'But if there's any time left after checking the other girls, we'll call you in.'

To my delight, I was called in and examined. Even though no trace of a baby was found, I felt so happy to have been treated the same as the other girls.

When the school term finished all the students from both the boys' school and the girls' school whose families lived in Nairobi travelled home on the bus together. This was another opportunity for the girls to be with their boyfriends. I used to sit and look at the couples flirting and cuddling each other and feel very left out. I tried to block out what was going on around me and to focus on how nice it would be to see my family again.

When I was 16 I was travelling back to Nairobi on the bus when a very handsome boy climbed aboard. I heard one of the girls whisper that he had just joined the boys' school. I had already sat down. He saw my face, grinned and sat down in the seat directly in front of mine. He introduced himself to me and told me his name was Peter.

'What's your name?' he asked.

'Anne Olympia.'

'Anne Olympia – what a cool name! How did you get a name like Olympia?'

'My dad looked at me when I was born and decided I was going to achieve great things so he gave me that name,' I giggled.

'I'm sure your dad will be proved right,' he replied.

As we chatted, it emerged that he came from a rich family. He asked me if I had a boyfriend. When I shook my head, his eyes lit up.

When the bus stopped for people to use the toilet and buy cold drinks, he said, 'Let's go and take a walk.'

'Let's just sit here instead,' I replied hurriedly. I was

sure that if he saw that I used callipers and crutches he
would lose interest immediately.

'OK, Anne Olympia, whatever you wish. We'll stay on
the bus.'

As the bus drove into Nairobi we arranged to meet for
a date the following weekend at Kenyatta University, just
a short distance away from the barracks.

'We can eat chicken and chips and drink soda,' he said.

This is what I'd heard my friends did on dates. I was
thrilled and trembled with excitement. Not only did I
have a date, I had got myself someone who was more
handsome and sophisticated than the other girls'
boyfriends.

When we reached the bus station my friends came to
help me get off the bus. As soon as I stood up, Peter saw
me struggle with my crutches and callipers. I watched
his face change from eager interest to a kind of revul-
sion. He almost physically recoiled from me.

'Don't worry, Peter. I'll see you around,' I said with
tears in my eyes.

Being able to predict what his reaction would be when
he saw my disability didn't make it hurt any less.

Towards the end of secondary school I became friendly
with a boy called Charles who attended the boys' school
next door. He did know all about my disability and didn't
seem to be put off by it. We had met at various school
functions and one day I received a letter from him.

Everyone was very excited for me. 'What does it say? What does it say?' they demanded.

I started reading it out and was very impressed by the fluid, romantic tone.

'Hello, is it me you're looking for?' it began. I didn't realise until much later that the whole thing was taken from a Lionel Richie song. My friends didn't realise either and all of them thought it was very cool and copied the same letter to their boyfriends. I was very excited to have received my first ever love letter.

Charles had a relative who was disabled and whom he was close to and so he understood disability and knew it didn't change who a person was. I was delighted that somebody I liked wanted to be with me because he liked me just the way I was.

I found some romantic quotes to send back to him. We started meeting up, but I rejected his amorous advances because I remembered what the teachers at Joyland had said about how easily boys could take advantage of us. Once again I thought of Grace. My strong Christian beliefs also made me keen to keep men at arm's length.

In the end poor Charles gave up.

Another reason why I didn't jump into his arms was because I was scared about having sex. Most girls are apprehensive about how things will be the first time, but I had the added anxiety of wondering how I would negotiate my disability if I did become intimate with a man. Nobody had ever discussed this with me, or offered me practical guidance.

After Charles, a few other boys approached me and sent me romantic letters, but I turned them all down. I still dreamed of meeting the perfect man, though, the kind described in all those Mills & Boon novels. I was sure that one day I would meet him and would fall in love on the spot. I was certain that when this knight in shining armour came into my life all my fears about sex and disability and having children would vanish as the two of us walked off into the sunset and lived happily ever after, surrounded by lots of plump, healthy babies that I had effortlessly given birth to.

Chapter Eight

Bachelor of Education

I completed my A-levels at Kereri and did quite well. My dad had always hoped that I would become a lawyer, but my grades weren't quite good enough for that. I did do well enough to get a place to study for a Bachelor of Education degree, though, and he seemed very content with that. He ran around the barracks telling anyone who would listen, 'My daughter is going to university. She's the first in the family to do this.'

I was keen to become a teacher and was very happy to be doing that course. I kept pinching myself and saying to myself, 'Anne, is it really true that you have managed to get all the way to university?' I felt very privileged to be among the few Kenyans who had the opportunity.

I was offered a place at the university in Nairobi, but the campus was so large and spread out that I thought I would never manage to get from one lecture to the next. Instead I accepted a place at Moi University in Eldoret.

The campus there was far smaller and the buildings much closer together.

'If I go to Nairobi University I won't reach the lectures until they're almost finished. At least if I go to Moi I might arrive in time to hear most of what the lecturer is saying,' I said to my dad.

'You could do with one of those motorised golf buggies, the kind you see in Hollywood movies,' my dad joked. 'Then you'd be first in line for all your lectures.'

Wheelchairs were rarely used in Kenya and were very difficult to get hold of, so I never even thought about trying to get one. Even if I had had one, the university was not wheelchair-accessible. Callipers and crutches were the standard solution to immobility caused by polio and the luckier ones struggled along in the same way that I did. The less fortunate crawled in the dust, using their arms to propel their lower body forwards, or devised makeshift boards on wheels which they perched on and rolled themselves through the streets.

Getting around on callipers and crutches wasn't getting any easier for me, however. At Kereri I had developed systems so that I didn't need to walk too far. My friends had fetched things for me and most of my lessons had been in one place. Now I was starting all over again in a new place and was filled with the same sense of hopelessness that I had felt when I started at secondary school.

I told my dad I didn't feel I would be able to manage at university.

'Anne, you will find a way to overcome any problems in your path just as you have always done before,' he said reassuringly. 'Don't think of the problems, focus on your achievements. It isn't easy for anyone to get to university, but you have succeeded.'

'We'll see,' I said doubtfully.

Although Moi University was smaller than Nairobi University, it still seemed huge to me. It was a collection of modern buildings and had running water and electricity along with a well-stocked library and pleasant gardens where students could sit and relax.

There were three different cafeterias that we called the 'mess'. The first time I went to one of them it was raining and I slipped and fell in the mud. A male student who told me his name was Mike helped me get up, picked my crutches up and helped me to get to the cafeteria. He bought me a cup of tea and told me that he loved to play the guitar. I told him that I played keyboards and we agreed to meet up to play and sing together. He seemed a very nice person and I was happy that something good had come out of falling over.

Although I was determined to start Moi with a positive attitude, daily life was, as I had suspected, a real struggle. I was constantly late for lectures, especially those that were back to back. The other students used to run from one lecture to the next, but of course I couldn't do that.

The students were very kind, though, and when I missed parts of lectures they gave me their notes afterwards so that I could catch up. A couple of girls from my old school were at the university and it was nice to see some familiar faces. Thankfully, too, I didn't get the same kind of stares from my fellow students that I had endured at Kereri.

I was grateful for the kindness and practical support I received, but unfortunately it didn't help me to move around any more quickly. The library was out of bounds to me because it was a mile away from the hostel where I was staying.

When I first arrived it was the rainy season and that made things particularly difficult for me. Staying upright became even more of a precarious business than it was when the earth was dry and dusty beneath my feet. When it rained I slipped and slid like a child experimenting with roller skates for the first time. I fell often and was constantly covered in bruises. The furthest I could manage to walk was 100 metres at a snail's pace. After that I would have to rest.

Whenever I felt I couldn't take another step I gave myself a stern pep talk: 'Come on, Anne, you can do it. Don't give up now, you're almost there. You know you'll be angry with yourself if you give up before you reach your destination. Don't forget how privileged you are to be here.'

Usually through sheer effort of will I managed to find the strength to complete my journey.

I shared a room with a lovely girl called Catherine who was very supportive of me. We talked about everything under the sun and became like sisters because of the amount of time we spent together.

I struggled to wash my clothes, so my friends did them for me, and when everyone's clothes had dried it was my job to fold and sort them all. I felt much happier making a contribution than just having everything done for me.

My friends also agreed to fetch books from the library for me so that was at least one arduous journey I didn't have to make. Although there was running water at the university it wasn't near the bathroom area, so I was dependent on them to bring water for me as well.

But even with my friends' support I felt that daily life was very hard. The distances I had to cover every day meant that I was in a perpetual state of physical exhaustion. I devoted so much energy to getting myself to the lectures that I had few reserves left to concentrate on listening to my lecturers and writing essays. I knew that my dad would be terribly disappointed if I gave up, but I started to feel that university just wasn't a realistic prospect for a girl like me.

I made an appointment with the vice-chancellor to tell him that I was going to quit. I entered his plush office with trepidation and despairingly informed him of my plans.

'If all I had to do was sit in lectures and write essays I'd be very happy to continue my studies,' I said to him.

'But I'm finding it too hard to get around the campus. I think it's time for me to quit. I've been late for almost every lecture.'

The vice-chancellor listened to me thoughtfully and then got up and invited me to sit in his upholstered leather chair. I had no idea what his point was, but I obediently got off my much more humble chair and got myself round to the other side of his desk. His chair was the softest and most comfortable I had ever sat on.

'How does that feel?' he asked.

'It's very comfortable,' I replied.

'Well, if you believe in yourself, Anne, you will be sitting in better seats than this one. I know that things are hard for you, but good things come to those who wait. I believe that your intellect is too good for you to throw away this opportunity. Somehow you have to carry on with your studies here. I believe you have a great future ahead of you.'

As I listened to his inspiring words I thought, 'Why is he telling me all this? He doesn't have a disability, so he doesn't know how hard it is. Anybody can utter fine words, but what would really make a difference to me is some practical help.'

I could see that his intentions were good, though, and I felt that he was speaking to me with the love of a father.

One concession that he did make for me was that I no longer needed to queue up for food but could go straight to the kitchen and eat there. This did make a difference, but the rest of my mobility problems remained.

Nevertheless I decided to try to carry on at Moi. I continued to fall over but tried my best to ignore these tumbles. Somehow I adapted. What really helped was that so many people around me supported me.

There was a blind girl called Alice who was in some of the same classes as me. She had lost her sight as a result of measles, another avoidable disease.

I asked her, 'What's it like to be blind?'

'What's it like not to be able to walk?' she replied.

We used to sit and laugh about our respective disabilities. One day I had to guide her to a place she needed to go on my callipers and crutches. We collapsed into giggles because I was such a useless guide. Another time she tried on my lipstick and looked hilarious because she couldn't see to put it on properly.

I started to think about disability in a different way. Here was someone with the use of her legs, but her legs weren't so useful to her without her eyes. Although I couldn't dance the way she could, she couldn't see the beautiful colours of the world.

I became her eyes, but unfortunately she couldn't become my legs when I needed to get from one place to another.

'Give me your legs and I'll go and run in the valley,' I said.

'Give me your eyes and I'll go pick out some beautiful clothes,' she replied.

I became interested in finding out more about the situation for people with disabilities in other countries and conducted some research. I was astounded to see the lengths some countries had gone to to support people with disabilities. In many Western countries there were people with disabilities who acted as role models. I wasn't aware of any disabled role models in Kenya. As far as I knew there was no one whose footsteps I could strive to follow in.

While I struggled to get through each day, I adored my studies. I was surrounded by intellectuals and for the first time felt that I really was on an equal footing with able-bodied people.

I enjoyed the small discussion groups that the students organised for themselves. The subjects were incredibly varied, ranging from the Napoleonic wars to the phonetics of Swahili.

Mike and I also started a contemporary gospel group at the university. He left after a year to retrain as a pastor at a theological college, but we stayed in touch and I played keyboards as backing for an album he and his family were recording.

I continued to sing and made friends with some girls who also loved to sing. We decided to form a group. Sometimes we performed at Christian rallies. We even got requests to perform at weddings.

One evening we were invited to perform at the vice-chancellor's home. He lived in a beautiful house with lovely carpets and fine china. After we had eaten, we sang for him and his family. Most of his children were grown up, but he had also adopted a young boy. I could see that this boy had found a home full of love and happiness.

As time went by I blossomed at Moi. University really built up my confidence. The fact that people rarely stared at me helped me to grow stronger and I developed a sense of self-worth. I felt good when I could triumph in the intellectual discussions we had and proud when I appeared in front of 2,000 people singing or playing keyboards. At those times people were looking at me because they admired my skills, not because they thought I was a freak who deserved pity.

I enjoyed life to the full and embraced all the opportunities that were open to me. I was determined not to let anything stand in the way of getting my degree. But the happiest times were those when I didn't feel disabled.

The university was generally a peaceful place. Although tribal conflict is a fact of life in Kenya, students from many different tribes got along well there. You could tell by people's facial features, names and surnames what tribe they were from, but it never became a source of discord. Luos, Luhyas and Kikuyus are the three biggest tribes in the country. Tribalism has damaged Kenyan society and slowed down the country's development, but generally speaking, educated people are less likely to get entrenched in tribal conflict.

Occasionally, though, trouble spilled onto the campus from outside. One time members of the Kikuyu and Kalenjin tribes who lived close to the university were fighting over land and both tribes surrounded the university and began firing their bows and arrows at each other.

Everyone was terrified at being caught up in this senseless violence. Things became so bad that the bus drivers didn't want to carry passengers from one tribe in case it caused them trouble when they passed through a rival tribal area. There had been cases of a bus travelling through a particular tribal area being forced to stop and any passengers from a rival tribe being dragged off and killed.

The university tried to remain neutral when the tribal conflicts raged around their perimeter.

When I witnessed these bitter feuds I wished that everyone was intermarried in the hope of diluting the tension. My brothers and sisters did not marry along tribal lines; in fact they found partners from so many different backgrounds that we joked our family was like the UN.

Tribal conflict wasn't the only problem I witnessed while I was at university. On one occasion the students themselves rioted in protest at some of the conditions at the university. My friends and I had heard rumours that a riot was being planned and one day some of the boys we described as 'rowdy' came to my room. They warned me to leave early the following day before the trouble started. I had no idea where I was supposed to go to.

Sure enough, the riot began the next day. I peered out of the window of my room and could see lots of running and screaming and broken glass. I was absolutely terrified. What on earth had possessed these people to turn to violence and destruction? I now realised that violence wasn't something that only happened along tribal lines but an ugly aspect of human nature which found many different excuses to show its face.

A few of my friends and I crept out of our rooms and went to hide in the lecturers' quarters, where we thought we'd be a bit safer. We went to the home of a female lecturer and found many other students hiding there.

One of the rioting students was shot by a police officer and the police cleared everyone out of the campus to try and regain control of the place.

My friends Helen, Ann and Catherine walked off the campus with me to seek refuge in a nearby village. Because I couldn't run, the police took all of us in their car to the main gate.

Everywhere had been wrecked. The students had smashed doors, windows, bunk beds and desks. For me, these terrifying scenes brought back awful memories of the coup.

'You can come and sleep in our home for tonight, but we don't have much,' one family in the village offered. I slept there in my callipers with my crutches by my side.

I was too scared to remove my callipers in case the fighting spread and we had to leave quickly. I wanted to be ready to run, psychologically at least. But I woke up screaming in agony because callipers are not supposed to be left on around the clock. Catherine tried her best to massage my swollen legs.

We had to move on because it wasn't safe to stay in the village for too long. The next day we got a bus to Nairobi. Helen's dad came to meet us there and drove me to the barracks.

The university was closed for more than six months for repairs and I was very sad to be missing my studies. When we did return, every student was fined 6,000 Kenyan shillings, whether they'd been involved in the protest or not. I was very upset at having to pay out for something I'd not been part of.

I had remained close to my grandmother, although I didn't get to see her very often. She had been present at my birth and had keenly followed my progress throughout my life. Along with my mum, she had done everything possible to keep me alive after I contracted polio and had defended me against the cruel taunts of the villagers, showering me with fierce, protective love.

By the time she was nearing the end of her life, her hair had grown down to her thighs. She plaited it into dreadlocks and every so often she unplaited it, washed it and then laid her head in my lap while I oiled it for her.

She had various tribal tattoos – lines carved into her forehead, her cheeks, her neck and her breasts – which were regarded as a sign of beauty.

She also had a hole under her lip and wore a round piece of polished wood through it like some kind of giant earring. When she took it out and sipped drinks, the liquid dribbled out through the hole under her lip.

When I said that wearing lipstick was a sign of beauty she was scornful, saying that it was just temporary paint while she had lasting signs of beauty on her body. I realised that there were many different perceptions of beauty.

My grandmother always swathed herself in white clothes, a sign of holiness. She was famous in the village for the huge bunches of bananas she carried gracefully on her head. Although she was slight, she was extremely strong. I loved being able to go home and buy her little luxuries like new clothes, sugar and cooking oil. She believed that drinking tea was a sin and instead used to fry sugar to turn it brown, then mix it with milk and hot water.

The last time I saw her was just before I graduated. She burst into tears of joy when she saw me and started dancing around me and jumping up and down, more like an excited child than a woman in her eighties.

'Anne, you've grown so beautiful,' she said, 'and you're such a clever girl, going to university and doing so well. People in this village didn't believe you'd amount to much after you became ill, but I knew what a special child you were. When your father gave you the name

Olympia he understood that you would go far in life. I knew that too.'

She started spitting on me – the traditional way in our village of giving a child blessings. Then she knelt down and thanked God and started calling the names of dead relatives to tell them the good news about how I'd turned out.

'I'm going to take the good news with me when I die,' she said, clapping her hands joyfully together.

Watching her blessing me in this way made me feel very emotional. My eyes filled with tears. It was wonderful to feel so loved.

The last words she said to me were, 'No matter where you go, God has got you in His palm. Never, ever ask Him why He took away your legs. He has bestowed many rich gifts upon you, my child.'

A few weeks after I left the village she fell while carrying water from the river. She was taken to hospital and passed away there.

I cried many tears when I heard that she'd gone. She had been so full of life when I last saw her and it was my dream that when I'd graduated and got a job I would bring her to live with me and make her final days really comfortable.

At least she had lived a long and healthy life. Life in the village was the only one she knew and maybe it would have been a mistake to uproot her and transplant her into unfamiliar surroundings.

* * *

Back on campus there were lots of romances and quite a few pregnancies. Some of the students who shared my Christian faith expressed interest in me.

My own heart beat faster whenever I was in the company of my friend Andrew. We had been friends for a long time. He was a kind and gentle human being. When it rained, he held an umbrella up for me because he knew it was impossible for me to juggle one with my crutches. He used to call into my room sometimes at the end of the day and say, 'I've come to say hello and goodnight.' When he was around I felt I was fizzing like a bottle of soda.

I confided in my friend Catherine that I had feelings for Andrew.

'It's so obvious it's mutual,' she said. 'You two would make a great couple.'

'Oh, I'm sure he just wants to be friends,' I said. But I fervently hoped I was wrong about that.

Andrew always dressed smartly and behaved in the same thoughtful, courteous way as all the Mills & Boon heroes I'd read about. Could he be the Mr Right I'd dreamed of for so long?

Catherine and I chatted and giggled about him long into the night. She was so excited for me and just wanted me to be happy.

'He's a good person,' she said, 'and so are you. He'll look after you and you can look after him.'

One evening Andrew and I arranged to meet on a bench close to my room. He seemed nervous and took my hand as soon as we'd sat down.

'Anne, I've observed you for a long time,' he said. 'There are so many things I like about you. I would love to be with you.'

A huge smile spread across my face.

'Oh, Andrew, I feel the same way about you. I would love to be with you,' I replied. My heart was banging excitedly against my chest.

'I want us to go out together and get engaged,' he continued, encouraged by my obvious enthusiasm for him.

'Oh yes, that would make me very happy,' I said. I was smiling so broadly I thought the skin of my cheeks might split.

'Anne Wafula, you're the luckiest girl in the world,' I said to myself.

We hugged each other, incredibly relieved that everything was now out in the open. Then we started making plans, talking about how our wedding would be, where we would live and how many children we would have. I prayed that now I had found the right man, God would give me the babies I longed for.

That night I was too happy to sleep.

I assumed I'd see Andrew around the campus the next day, but curiously he seemed to have disappeared.

I couldn't understand what had gone wrong. Had I done something foolish without realising?

A couple of days later, a fat envelope was pushed under my door. I knew without opening it that it was a letter from Andrew.

As I read it, tears splashed onto Andrew's neat handwriting. The letter told me of how much he loved me and of his family's refusal to allow the relationship to go ahead because of my disability. He tried to find a kind way of saying that his family didn't consider me good enough for their son.

'I'm too devastated about the whole thing to even look you in the eye, Anne,' he wrote.

I had heard that his family were wealthy and controlling, and wondered how the conversation had gone. Maybe his father had said, 'Andrew, you can do better than marrying a cripple.' And perhaps his mother had presented an able-bodied girl to him and suggested that he married her instead, a girl he didn't know or love the way he loved me but someone who was much more suitable because her legs worked.

Andrew was the first boy I had truly loved. It was one thing to lose a man because he had fallen in love with someone else, but this was something completely different. Society and its stupid values were denying two people the chance of a lifetime of happiness together just because a virus had randomly swept through my body a couple of decades before. Life really was unjust.

I felt low for a very long time. I was prepared to struggle twice as hard just to be treated the same as able-bodied people, I was prepared to make the best of everything and was determined not to dwell on my disability or to feel sorry for myself, but this was too bitter a blow. I felt that no matter what I did, society

would never stop shrieking, 'Disabled!' at me. All I
wanted was to be left in peace and to compete on an
equal footing with those who could walk. My dad had
always told me that education was the key to a good life.
But clearly it wasn't enough.

I had been so looking forward to graduating, but now
the whole thing had lost its appeal for me. I longed to
have Andrew by my side to share this achievement with.

My friends tried their best to comfort me. They were
very supportive and they did make me feel valued and
loved. But I knew this was something I wouldn't recover
from quickly.

Once you have graduated as a teacher, the government
allocates a school for you to work in. A couple of weeks
later I received an admission letter to one of the top
schools in Nairobi to teach history and Swahili. This
really lifted my spirits. I couldn't have landed myself a
more prestigious teaching job.

But once again my joy was short-lived. When the
school found out that I was disabled, they withdrew the
job offer, saying that they did not have the facilities to
cater for a person in my condition. Yet again I had been
cast aside for no good reason.

Some of my friends suggested that I apply to teach at
a school for the physically handicapped. But I refused.

'Why should I do that?' I asked. 'I don't want to hide
away in a world of disability. I'm just as good as the

other teachers who have graduated. I don't want to be treated like a special case.'

I rarely said 'Why me?' about my disability. I had a reputation among my friends and lecturers for cheerfulness and a determination not to be defeated by any obstacle that laid itself across my path. But that night as I lay sobbing into my pillow I wished with all my heart that the polio virus had never entered my body.

Chapter Nine

A Proper Job

I graduated from Moi University with a Bachelor of Education degree at the end of 1994. My dad was coming up to retirement from the army and had a lot of handing-over work to do, so unfortunately he couldn't come along to my graduation ceremony. Many students themselves didn't attend; some couldn't afford the expense and others had already got jobs. I felt very proud when I was handed my certificate with a wax seal on it. I thought back to how I had almost given up on my degree during the first few weeks. Thank goodness I had stuck with it. Although I had had some tough times, holding this certificate in my hand and knowing that I could now get a good job made it all worthwhile. I also received a student merit award for being the most 'enduring and sociable' student in the years 1990–1994.

Modelling was not a career I had ever envisaged for myself, but a few weeks after graduation I went to visit my sister Jane in Nairobi and was waiting at a bus stop with a friend when I noticed that a man with a camera was also standing in the queue and looking at me intently.

'Are you in pain?' he asked, pointing to my callipers and crutches.

I was taken aback, because I wasn't used to such direct approaches.

'It's pain I can bear,' I replied and smiled.

'Listen, I work for a fashion magazine and I think you have a really beautiful face. Would you allow me to take your photo? It will appear soon in the magazine.'

I shrugged, unsure whether or not he was serious. My friend and I even started laughing at the idea of a disabled girl in a fashion magazine. It wasn't the kind of image that usually featured.

'Oh well, why not?' I said.

The man asked me to smile and look natural, took a few photos there and then and told me to look out for them in the magazine in the next few weeks.

Sure enough, a feature appeared with the headline 'Beautiful daughters of Kenya'.

The photographer's assignment had involved taking pictures of ordinary young women on the streets of Kenya. All the other girls were pictured posing in short skirts, but in my case they only showed my face.

I was proud of the photo, but I was disappointed that they had hidden my disability by not showing my whole body. I wanted people to see that beauty and disability could go together. Still, after my recent disappointments the photo gave me a much-needed confidence boost.

My sister Jane was heavily pregnant with her first child and looked stunning in a maternity dress I'd bought her. I looked at her swollen belly and longed for it to be transferred to me. I imagined how overjoyed I would be if I had a reason to wear a maternity dress.

'Ahh, I'm tired, Anne,' she complained. 'The baby dances in my stomach all night and keeps me awake.'

How I wished that I could be in her shoes, being kept awake by my baby kicking in my womb. The community saw my sister as a complete woman and I knew they would never look at me that way. It made me feel very sad.

I cheered up when I was offered a job at Machakos Technical Training Institute, about 45 minutes' drive from Nairobi. The college was an alternative to university for students who wished to acquire vocational and practical skills. Sometimes people already in employment would be sent there to update their skills.

My dad was so proud when I told him about the job. Whenever I told him about the disappointments in my life he always brushed them aside, saying that they weren't important and that I was going to make a big success of my life. He was so confident in my abilities that he wasn't prepared to have his belief in me dented by what he considered to be minor setbacks. He himself had been a teacher before he joined the army and he was particularly pleased that I was following in his footsteps.

By the time I started teaching he had retired from the army and gone back to the village. He had always been determined to move back to his ancestral land, regardless of the fact that villagers had urged my mother and grandmother to do away with me and thought we were cursed.

'Showing them what a success you have become is the best way to challenge these prejudices,' he said.

Now he strolled from hut to hut, saying to anyone who would listen, 'Look at Anne, she's a teacher now. She's a university graduate, you know, the first in the family.'

Very few people in the village had acquired university degrees and I know that my dad took particular pleasure in boasting about my achievements.

I was contracted to teach history, Swahili and communication skills. When I went to meet the college principal for the first time I noticed that he shook hands with me using his left hand, although custom dictated that the right was used.

'Welcome to Machakos Technical College,' he said. 'I had no idea that you were disabled,' he continued cheerfully.

I held my breath, worrying that he too would decide to reject me on the basis of disability, but he actually seemed encouraged by it.

Then I noticed that his right hand was withered and presumed that this was why he wasn't using it.

'Ahh, are you wondering why my hand looks like this?' he asked, smiling. 'I had polio as a child and it left me with this paralysed arm. The teachers used to try and make me write with this hand, but eventually they gave up and let me use my left.'

I smiled in recognition and felt excited. I was sorry that he had had polio but I couldn't help also being pleased. It was the first time I had seen anyone with the same disability as me achieve such high office. I was sure that I would be happy and supported at this college and I felt inspired in the principal's company.

'Did you have polio too?' he asked.

I nodded vigorously.

'Well, I'm delighted to see that you didn't let it hold you back,' he replied.

I vowed that I would work as hard as he had so that I could achieve what he had achieved.

'Anne, you are very young, but I can see that you're going to make a very good teacher,' he said.

'Thank you, but I feel very nervous,' I admitted. 'It's such an important job and I don't know how the students will respond to me. I hope that they won't take advantage of me because of my callipers and crutches.'

'I'm sure you'll assert your authority in the same way as other teachers and that you'll soon have the students eating out of your hand,' he said.

'I struggle to move very far on my callipers and crutches,' I confessed.

'Don't worry, we have some teachers' accommodation very close to the classrooms and you can move in there. I think it will make life much easier for you,' he smiled.

My new living quarters were perfect – a sitting room, a bedroom and a little bathroom. I was overjoyed when I saw how clean and comfortable it was. The bathroom would be much more pleasant for me to use than the ones at Kereri and the university. It was also the first time in my life that I had had a place of my own. I knew that many other girls went straight from living with their family or in a boarding-school dormitory to living in their husband's family home. I felt as if I'd arrived at the Ritz.

My sister Jane gave me her own bed so that I wouldn't have to sleep on a mattress on the floor. I was very grateful to her and felt lucky that I came from such a close and loving family where we all cared about each other and tried to help each other out.

And so began my life at Machakos. A house girl called Mary came to help me with cooking and other domestic tasks. Everything was organised for me and at last I felt as if all my troubles were over. I had worked hard to overcome all the obstacles in my path and I had achieved my dream of getting a good job, leading an independent life and giving something back to the community.

On my first day of teaching the principal introduced me to all the students at assembly. 'I'd like you all to meet Miss Wafula,' he said. I was so thrilled to hear him say 'Miss Wafula' that I momentarily forgot that my dress had snagged on my crutches and ridden up. I couldn't let go of them to pull it down otherwise I would have fallen over in front of everybody, a humiliation I was sure I would never live down. So instead I stood there, hoping that nobody would notice. After that first day I made sure I always wore long skirts or trousers to teach in to avoid a repeat performance of 'hitched up syndrome'.

After assembly I was told to fill in a form so that my payslips could be processed. I noted with delight that there was no box to tick stating that I had a disability. As far as the accounts department at Machakos Technical College was concerned, I was just another member of staff who needed to be paid.

Teachers in Kenya are held in very high regard and I always felt I had a big responsibility to support my students and make sure they did well. At first I was very nervous standing up in front of them. I was a similar age to some of them, so it was hard for me to lay down boundaries.

Some of them took advantage of my youth and disability. One time I was teaching them about exam technique and general knowledge. As I struggled to remain upright and write on the board, one of the students wolf-whistled.

I turned round as quickly as I was able to on my callipers and crutches.

'Who whistled?' I asked sternly.

Nobody answered.

I walked into the centre of the class trying my best to look authoritarian, but slipped and fell – not the best way to control the class.

I picked myself up and tried to look composed, although I was on the verge of bursting into tears, and repeated loudly, 'Who whistled?'

Again there was silence.

'I'm not leaving the class until you tell me who whistled,' I said icily.

Nobody spoke.

'OK. You've left me with no choice but to alert the principal,' I said.

I struggled out of the room, thankful that his office was not too far away.

'You've done the right thing by speaking to me about this, Anne,' he said sympathetically. 'You can't let the students get away with that kind of impertinence or they'll become unteachable. I'm going to suspend them all from classes until the person who disrespected you by wolf-whistling confesses.'

After that one of the boys confessed and was suspended for a while.

I didn't like taking such a tough line, but knew it was the only way for me to control my class. I earned the respect of the students and nobody misbehaved after that.

Although I grew to love teaching, as usual my biggest problem was getting from one class to another. Living so close to my classes made a big difference, but I struggled whenever I had to navigate steps. Each one felt like going up or down a mountain.

After each day of teaching I was completely exhausted. I would go home, remove my callipers and slump into a deep, dreamless sleep.

Callipers and crutches enabled me to get around, but they had many shortcomings. My armpits turned black from having the crutches propped into them and I constantly suffered from boils which got infected and reinfected as the crutches and callipers chafed against my skin. I was forever dousing myself with iodine, but only put it on at night because I didn't want to drive the students away with the pungent smell during classes.

I loved the school holidays because I could sit in my house and do very little walking or standing. Mary, my house help, was very loyal and kind and she made my life so much easier.

I also got to know a teacher called Margaret who had an autistic son. She became a friend and mentor to me. She was very generous-spirited and praised my work at every opportunity. She loved her son very much and it reminded me of how much my mum had loved me. At moments like that I still felt her loss keenly.

Sometimes Margaret took me to the market and selected beautiful clothes for me. It made all the difference to be surrounded by people who helped and supported me.

I did still encounter prejudice, though. Someone who knew my sister Vicky visited me once. I had never liked her, but she took my breath away when she started insulting me and calling me a cripple in my own house. I wondered where all this hatred and hostility was coming from. Was she annoyed because I had made a success of my life, thinking that as a person with a disability I didn't deserve success and happiness?

At one point she shouted at me and then pushed me sharply.

'Please don't push me into a corner. You're hurting me,' I said calmly, hoping to diffuse her rage.

'So what do you think you can do, cripple?'

I became enraged at her continual use of the word and wished she would just leave my house. In desperation I tried to push her away with my crutch and caught her lip with it, making it bleed.

'Please don't bleed on my floor. Wipe it up and go,' I said coldly.

She left my house, saying, 'Don't ever play with that cripple, she's too strong.'

I felt defiled by her presence in my home. It shook me to the core to be confronted by such naked prejudice and hatred. How could someone feel such strong antipathy towards me because I had been permanently damaged by a virus?

Fortunately, I was surrounded by a nice group of teachers. The college was a good, friendly place to work and I felt that the principal set the tone for everyone else's behaviour.

I became friendly with one of the teachers called Paul, who taught secretarial skills. He kept smiling across the staff room at me and made it clear that he fancied me. I wondered if at last, at 24 years old, I was going to have my first proper boyfriend.

He invited me to go with him to a nice hotel nearby for a meal. We ate chips in the hotel restaurant, fashionable date food at the time because it was Western rather than African, and chatted about school matters. Things never went any further, though, because he wasn't sure whether or not I would refuse him if he asked me out.

I was disappointed, because I liked Paul, but I kept on saying to myself that when I met the right person I would just know. Although in some ways I lacked confidence, I did have a sturdy core of self-belief and it was not the done thing in Kenya for morally upstanding people to have too many girlfriends or boyfriends, so I didn't worry too much about my lack of a relationship. Mid-twenties was the time when educated people started to think about marriage, and people with good jobs were considered a better catch. I was mixing in educated circles and hoped that sooner or later I would meet my Mr Right – a variation on the Mills & Boon heroes I was so familiar with. And as soon as I found this perfect man, I would get married and have children.

Whenever I thought about having children, though, Grace's death in childbirth came into my head. I decided to consult a doctor to see if it was physically possible for me to get pregnant and give birth to a baby.

The doctor's assessment wasn't encouraging: 'You have no stomach muscles and your cervix hasn't developed properly. It's crooked, and one side of your pelvis is bigger than the other because of the polio. Even if you did conceive it would be very hard for you to carry a child.'

I left the doctor's consulting room feeling devastated. I couldn't imagine waking up childless every day for the rest of my life. Children are a very important part of African society and women who can't bear children are often looked down on. I was determined not to give up hope, though, and decided that if the doctor was right I would consider adoption, because I knew there were many orphans in desperate need of a good home.

I became friendly with a man called Mark, who was a lawyer and a part-time teacher at the college. Once again lots of the teachers kept telling me that he fancied me. He invited me to go to Nairobi with him and when we arrived there he presented me with a huge bunch of red roses.

'Oh, thank you,' I gasped. 'Nobody has ever bought me red roses before. I used to read a lot of Mills & Boon books as a teenager and the hero always gave the girl roses.'

We both laughed.

Mark never said outright that he was interested in me, but even if he had declared his love I didn't feel he was the right man for me. Eventually, when he started practising law, he moved to a different town, but we remained friends.

After that I had a relationship with a man who lived locally that didn't work out. It left me feeling bruised and suspicious of men.

As time went by I developed good relationships with some of the students. They realised that I had had to work extra hard to become a teacher and they felt that because I'd obviously struggled myself, I'd be sympathetic to their troubles. I developed a reputation as the college agony aunt as more and more students came to me and confided their problems. Once they got to know me properly, they started to confide in me about private matters like being infected with HIV.

One student told me that she had been raped a few years before she'd arrived at the college. The rapist had left her pregnant, but she had gone on to lose the baby. A couple of years later she had started to get ill. She had not had any other relationships since the rape and suspected that the rapist had infected her with HIV. I was so sorry to hear what had happened to her. She used to come to my house and I would give her fruit and vegetables or a glass of milk, the kind of things she wasn't getting in the school dining room.

HIV was an alarmingly common problem among the students and I realised that it was a new kind of disability, one that was swathed in stigma, just like polio. Because I had suffered so much stigma myself, I didn't want to see others going through it.

At that time HIV was a relatively new subject for discussion in Kenya. When I was at secondary school I had known very little about it because it was so rarely discussed. My only experience of it had been when I'd met a woman who had come to Kenya from the Democratic Republic of Congo as a refugee. She was a neighbour of some of my friends from primary school and I saw her from time to time when I was at secondary school. She found a job as a secretary, but then became ill. At first it hadn't seemed serious: she had simply developed a small blister on her finger. By the next time I saw her it had grown much bigger, though, and by the time after that it had devoured her whole finger. It seemed that she was quite literally being eaten alive.

When I asked her what was the matter with her, she said she was suffering from the same disease as Rock Hudson. I didn't know who he was and had no idea what she was talking about. The next time I went to see her I was told that she had got much sicker – she had become emaciated and her whole body had been covered in blisters – and that she had gone home to die.

At that time information was just starting to circulate publicly about this potentially fatal condition.

Information films were screened on the television, but many people were in denial and didn't want to engage with the taboo that HIV was spread by having sex. Instead they said that AIDS was a curse and if you found a way to purge yourself of it you could survive.

When the students started confiding in me about their HIV status, I decided that it was time for me to find out more about this terrible illness. I did some research about how it was transmitted and then gave talks at some of the disability forums in the area. These forums had been set up so that disabled people could offer support to each other. I felt that people with disabilities would be particularly vulnerable to sexual exploitation, which could lead to them being infected with HIV.

I began to understand how many different ways there were to be disabled. AIDS was a disability that was killing many people. It was time for me to expand my definition of the word 'disability'. On the outside a person could be able-bodied and nicely dressed, with strong arms and strong legs, and yet beneath that robust exterior all kinds of things could be going on in their body and mind. I looked at my weak legs and was grateful that at least I had a strong heart inside me.

I always tried to make the best of what I had and not to cry for things I didn't have. I realised that the greatest differences between people are not who is disabled and who is not, but how we choose to deal with the situations we are faced with. I had no control over getting polio, but did have control over how I lived my life and what I achieved. And the freedom to choose which path to take was the most precious thing of all.

Chapter Ten

Not Quite Mills & Boon

At a function for special needs children at Margaret's son's school I met an Englishwoman called Justine who was working for the charity Voluntary Service Overseas. Through her I got to know a few of the other volunteers in the area. Sometimes when they came to town to do their shopping they popped in to see me, watched videos on my video player and television and used my toilet and shower – luxuries they didn't have in the villages where they were volunteering. It was interesting for me to meet people from a different culture and to see how they lived.

I was feeling very buoyant at this time. I had got over my failed romance and was very focused on my career. There was a research centre in Machakos and many of the professors there had studied for their masters in Australia. They had recommended it highly as a place for post-graduate studies and told me it was a wonderful country, so I had applied to go to Brisbane University to study educational psychology and had been offered a place. I had never travelled outside Kenya and the idea of studying on another continent excited me. My confidence had grown and I felt equal to any challenge that life might throw in my path.

My dad was very keen for me to do the course. 'When you have a master's degree under your belt you will really be part of our country's elite,' he told me. 'You will be able to do anything you wish. Remember, I've always said that you're destined for great things.'

I was making my preparations to leave Kenya when everything changed forever.

It was August 1998 and my mind was buzzing with my Australia plans when I went along to a barbecue for one of the volunteer VSO teachers. Quite a few of them were there and some of the white women there were wearing short skirts and smoking. Although I'd seen this behaviour before from Western volunteers, it was hard for me to get used to it. Respectable Kenyan women didn't do that sort of thing. After my one experiment with smoking at Joyland, I had never touched a cigarette again. I wondered how much damage they were doing to their lungs.

As usual I was propped upright by my callipers and crutches, although my callipers were carefully hidden from view by the long flowing dress I was wearing. I had been wearing them for more than two decades now, but had never fully accepted them as a necessary extension to my body. I still loathed having them next to my skin. If only they could have been made of soft cotton wool rather than hard metal.

As I looked around the dim room, trying to work out who I knew, a white man approached me. He was balding and bespectacled and looked as if he was a generation ahead of me.

'Hello,' he said grinning. Then he gestured towards my crutches and said, 'Did you break your leg skiing?'

I gave him a frosty look. Was this what the English called humour? Was I supposed to be laughing at the absurd notion of snow in Kenya?

'No, I haven't broken my leg,' I said coldly. 'I had polio as a child.'

What an incredibly stupid man, I thought to myself, looking around the room to see if I could spot any of my friends.

I'd never seen anyone's face drop the way his did. He looked absolutely mortified at his blunder.

'I'm so sorry,' he said. 'Me and my big mouth. Please can I get you a drink by way of an apology?'

I nodded and he looked relieved.

'What would you like?'

'Just an orange juice, please. I don't drink alcohol.'

He brought me a drink and we found somewhere to sit outside and started chatting.

He told me that his name was Norman and that he was English. I looked at him as he chatted. Apart from his piercing blue eyes, he had nothing at all in common with the Mills & Boon heroes I had been led to believe were the prototypes for all Englishmen. Also, I had met quite a few English people by then, but none who spoke like him and I was struggling to understand his accent. He told me that he was what was known as a Geordie, a person from the north-east of England. I had never heard this term and wondered if it was a kind of tribe, similar to the ones we had in Kenya.

He appeared to be chatting me up, but I wasn't impressed. My thoughts were full of my trip to Australia and there was no space in my mind for romance. Both my dad and I were saving hard to make sure I had enough money to complete the course. Every time I thought about returning to Kenya with a master's degree, or even a doctorate, a thrill rippled through my body. I thought about my humble origins and all the villagers who had said that my life wasn't worth anything. Eventually I became lost in my thoughts and didn't pay too much attention to what Norman was saying.

As the sun went down mosquitoes circled and started to bite, so we moved inside. Norman continued talking and I decided to mention my problem.

'We've heard the queen speak on television,' I told him, 'and I don't have any problem understanding her, but it sounds as if you're from a different country.'

Norman laughed. He had a warm, throaty chuckle that appealed to me. He told me that he came from a poor mining community where many people didn't have a good education and the destiny of all the men was to work down the pit. It didn't sound too different from the lot of many people in my village, who spent their lives farming small plots of land.

'I always loved books, though,' he explained, 'and from the age of seven I spent a lot of time at the local library. Though I ended up going down the mines myself, literature opened up many new worlds to me and my dream has always been to write.'

He told me that one of his all-time favourite books was a French classic, Emile Zola's *Germinal*, a harsh story of a coal-mining strike in northern France in the 1860s. 'I think I'm the only person who has read that book while actually sitting in a mine,' he laughed.

He explained that he had been actively involved in the 1984–85 miners' strike, something I had never heard of, although it was apparently a major event in the UK. He had written a book about his part in it and when he had lost his job as a miner after the strike he had retrained as a teacher, something he felt hadn't been open to him when he had been at school because he hadn't excelled academically.

I was impressed by his decision to make such a big change in his life. Like me, he had swum against the tide to achieve his goal. As teachers, we shared a desire to nurture the next generation, show them the many doors that education could unlock and encourage them to believe that they could achieve their dreams.

Norman had taught English in the UK for a few years and then, frustrated by the bureaucracy in the British system, had decided to take a break and to volunteer as a teacher with the VSO. He was currently working in a Muslim village called Takaungu near Mombasa, a place Kenya's former president, Jomo Kenyatta, regarded as the father of the nation, liked to visit when he went to the coast.

As we chatted, Norman gazed at me intently. Towards the end of the evening he leaned over and stroked my arm.

'You have very beautiful skin,' he said.

What's wrong with this man? He seems obsessed, I thought to myself.

'Thank you,' I said.

During the evening various people had come up to chat to me and at those times Norman had gone to talk to other people, but he kept returning to me as if he was some kind of a homing pigeon. He might have been look-ing for a relationship, but I certainly wasn't. At the end of the evening I ordered a taxi to get home.

'I'll escort you,' Norman said, jumping in beside me before I could tell him that I was perfectly alright by myself.

When the driver drew up outside my house, Norman gave me a hug.

'It's been great meeting you, Anne. I'd love to keep in touch with you,' he said.

I decided not to mention that I was due to leave for

Australia in a few months time. We exchanged phone numbers and agreed to meet up for a coffee if either of us ever happened to be in the other one's neighbourhood.

After that I didn't think too much about Norman and continued with my work and my travel preparations. A few days later, though, I received a very enthusiastic and flirtatious letter from him saying that he'd love to see me again.

I wrote back cautiously saying that I would really have to think very hard before getting involved with anyone at the moment. I explained that I had recently ended a relationship and didn't feel ready for another one.

But Norman wasn't prepared to give up on me. He kept on writing and told me he'd continually tried to call me but hadn't been able to get through. I think he thought I'd deliberately given him the wrong phone number, but in fact the phone networks in Kenya aren't good and it's not unusual not to be able to get through to people.

A few weeks after we first met, Norman returned to Machakos to see me. I'd never been pursued so intensely by a man. I had started to like him, but I still wasn't interested in getting involved in a relationship because my thoughts were focused on my imminent trip. I didn't even open a small part of my heart to him because I felt it would be unfair to both of us because I wasn't going to be in Kenya for much longer.

Also, he had explained to me that he had been married but was now divorced and had two grown-up daughters. I decided that he had too much baggage and that I should probably steer clear of him. I was determined to find myself a partner who was genuine, and I just didn't know whether he fitted the bill.

When Norman visited me the second time he was wearing a white T-shirt covered in blue washing-powder stains. He looked so comical I couldn't help myself and burst out laughing.

'Why are you dressed like that, Norman?' I said. I realised that he had soaked his T-shirt in Omo, a popular washing powder with a distinctive blue colour.

'I'm not good with clothes,' he said sheepishly. 'In England I just throw everything into the washing machine and things seem to come out clean.'

What a lazy culture, I thought to myself.

'Here in Kenya we know how to wash our clothes properly and make sure they are fresh and clean before we put them on,' I said. 'You look as if you put the whole box of Omo in with those clothes, but you should only use a small amount.'

'I thought that the more I put in, the cleaner the clothes would come out,' he replied.

I started laughing again. Why were so many men so useless when it came to domestic matters?

Also, Western clothes are highly prized in African countries. When I was a child, sometimes market day in Webuye was full of European cast-off clothes and was referred to as 'go down' day because people rummaged on the floor among the piles of old clothes. The shoppers were proud of their Western acquisitions, even if they didn't understand what they were worn for in their previous lives. I once saw a woman in a trouser suit that she had carefully washed and ironed then paraded proudly in in church. I was amused when I found out that it was actually worn as a prison outfit in the UK. Sometimes people wore pyjamas to church, not knowing that Westerners wore such clothes to sleep in. Western clothes, of any description, were deemed much finer than whatever was available locally. So it particularly upset me to see that Norman was ruining his beautiful clothes.

'Would you like to see how your clothes should be cleaned?' I asked him. 'Mary, my house help, and I can do a proper job for you.'

'That would be great,' he grinned.

We took all the clothes he had brought with him and washed them for him. We returned them to him the following day, carefully washed, dried and neatly folded. He couldn't believe how clean they looked.

'Where am I going wrong?' he said. 'I've obviously got a lot to learn about how to do laundry.'

Norman was clearly never going to be a domestic god, but when he opened his mouth to speak I admired him. He had principles and he was knowledgeable about many different things. There was something very unique about him and his originality really appealed to me.

Slowly, his determination to win my heart started to pay off. The more I got to know him, the more genuine his nature seemed to be. I began to understand his dry sense of humour and how intelligent he was. I felt that he was a good, kind and honest person.

True, he didn't have the outer beauty of a Mills & Boon character, but his inner beauty shone through more and more clearly as time went by. In fact he made me re-evaluate my own criteria for a boyfriend. I had always been attracted to handsome men before, but their personalities had sometimes been rather less appealing. I now knew what was more important. The Prince Charmings I had read about so often suddenly became hollow and irrelevant to me. What could be worse than being with a man who had nothing underneath his looks? Marrying physical beauty alone was a recipe for disaster, I decided.

Very slowly my liking and respect for Norman turned into love. No thunderbolt of desire had struck me when I had first set eyes on him, but I was increasingly glad about that. It had allowed a steady and reliable foundation to be built up and a real friendship to develop between us.

Norman regularly referred to his opening line to me with a shudder, but I now made a joke about it. His remorse for the blunder made me like him more.

A lot of our time together was spent laughing. Norman was so amusing and for me there was nothing more attractive than being with a man who could entertain me the way he did. He was also very sensitive and his feelings were easily hurt. I realised that just as he made me feel loved and good about myself, I needed to make sure that he felt loved and good about himself.

I told him that I was planning on going to Australia to study.

'Oh, that's great,' he said. 'It's good to be ambitious.'

After his second visit he continued to bombard me with letters, asking me to be his girlfriend. His brain told him I wouldn't accept him because of the age and cultural differences, but his heart ignored his head because he had fallen in love with me.

Eventually I gave in. Norman clearly wasn't going to go away and because I liked him so much I asked myself what was to be gained by continuing to spurn his advances. I wrote back to him and said, 'OK, go with your heart.'

I was still planning on going to Australia at that point. I was determined not to put my life on hold just because I'd decided to go out with Norman.

He was ecstatic that I'd agreed to start a relationship with him and returned as soon as he had time off to see me again. He had had a long journey and I was delighted to see him, but greeted him at the door with a formal handshake and asked him to return later as I was in the middle of a women's group meeting. I couldn't jump on him and kiss him, because it is not part of African culture. It wasn't possible for him to stay at my house either, as I hardly knew him, so I asked one of my colleagues if Norman could stay with him.

Once again his T-shirts were stained blue. When he saw me looking critically at his outfit, he hung his head.

'Sorry, Anne. I did try to improve my washing techniques,' he said.

Each day that I spent with him I had a deeper feeling in my bones, a certainty that Norman was the man for me. I disapproved of his casual, scruffy way of dressing – teachers in Kenya always dressed smartly – yet at the end of the day things like that didn't matter. I loved Norman just the way he was.

The courtship was conducted mostly by letter and phone call because we lived so far away from each other. Norman's letters were full of his love for me. 'I'll meet you in my dreams,' he wrote.

Although the passion by post sustained us, Norman was determined that we should spend some proper time together and arranged a little holiday for us by the sea, not too far from where he was teaching. It was agreed that I would also spend some time in the village where he was teaching.

I had never been so happy in my entire life. I felt as if my whole body was extra-alive. Although the movements of my body were limited, my soul was turning cartwheels.

I was filled with excitement as we boarded the bus from Machakos to Mombasa. I had never been on a proper holiday before and I knew that Norman would keep me entertained for the whole of our journey.

Unfortunately, things didn't run very smoothly. The bus broke down, which is not a particularly unusual occurrence in Kenya. Most passengers are philosophical about such inconveniences, but Norman got very agitated.

At first he applied English standards and assumed that another bus would be along shortly. But six hours later there was no sign of one.

He paced up and down and cursed under his breath.

The other passengers urged him to keep calm and relax. '*Haraka Haraka, Haina Baraka*, hurry, hurry has no blessings,' they kept saying to him.

I wasn't in a position to try and calm Norman down because I was feeling very unwell. I had been advised to take anti-malarial tablets for the trip to the coast and had taken one before we started our journey and then eaten some avocado while we were waiting for the next bus to arrive. The combination made me vomit.

When the other passengers saw me being sick they turned on Norman and said accusingly, 'What are you doing to our sister? Are you trying to poison her?'

The look on poor Norman's face as people surrounded him and started speaking fast in Swahili he couldn't understand was almost comical. Even though I felt ill, I couldn't help smiling. I told Norman what they were saying and he said exasperatedly, 'Why would I poison the person I love?'

'Don't worry about it, Norman,' I said. 'It's best not to get involved in an argument.'

We eventually got on another bus. The bus driver kept stopping and piling more and more people on. Every time the bus went over a bump people flew up towards the ceiling.

'What about health and safety?' Norman yelled.

I laughed again. Why did Norman think that his British standards would apply on a rickety bus in Kenya? It seemed that British people liked doing everything in a hurry and expected things to always run smoothly. Kenyans never expected things to run smoothly and didn't mind if they happened slowly.

We finally reached Mombasa very late at night. The wall of heat hit me as soon as we arrived. It was much hotter than Machakos.

We realised we'd missed the last bus back to Norman's village.

'Just chill out, Norm,' I said to him.

We found a hotel to stay at overnight and travelled to the village the following day.

'I don't think I'll ever get used to the pace of life here,' Norman grumbled. 'It's not the way I'm used to living.'

Even I had to admit that the culture on the coast was slower than in other parts of Kenya. People stopped you and asked how every member of your family was doing and how your animals were getting on and then you would have to go through all the same questions with them.

We arrived in the village the following day. It was a Muslim village inhabited by light-skinned people of Arab origin. The first thing that struck me was how many beautiful women were milling around. All of them seemed extremely attentive towards Norman and I suddenly felt very insecure. Why on earth had Norman chosen me when he was surrounded by so many able-bodied women with perfect limbs? There was one woman in particular who looked as if she really had her eye on him. She was clearly unhappy to see me.

I reassured myself by saying that what we had was true love. Norman had ignored all those beautiful girls because the one he loved was me. I felt that at last I was one of those heroines in the Mills & Boons novels. I wasn't a perfect creature to the rest of the world, but in Norman's eyes I was, and that was all that mattered.

The village didn't resemble my village at all. The dwellings, known as Swahili houses, were constructed of stone and had beautiful individually carved wooden doors. The poorer people lived in mud huts. The village seemed wealthy and had five mosques. It was right next to the coast and coral rocks had been brought from the shore area and squared into building bricks. A nearby mangrove swamp provided good-quality wood for the houses. Fishing was a major source of nourishment for the villagers. The men fished and the women brought the fish off the boats in big baskets carried on their heads.

The Giriama tribe dominated this area and it was the custom of the women to leave their breasts uncovered.

'Oh my goodness, Norm,' I said, 'this isn't how the women in my village dress, or rather don't dress.'

'Well,' he replied, 'this is the fashion round here.'

A woman who was feeding her child caught sight of Norman, put down her child mid-glug and ran up to him with her breasts flapping.

'*Tupe Peremende*, give us sweets,' she cajoled.

'I don't have sweets today. Maybe tomorrow,' Norman replied in his rudimentary Swahili.

Although there were several thousand people living in the village I never saw a single one who was disabled. I later discovered that this was because they were locked inside the houses. It broke my heart to hear how those people were suffering and denied life chances. I thought how easily that could have been my fate and how lucky I was to have escaped it.

I could see that some of the lithe young women looked genuinely baffled that Norman had chosen a woman whose legs didn't work over one of them. But attitudes were not only negative towards people with disabilities. The unmarried women, the divorcées and the single mums were also stigmatised, and the work they did reflected this. Suicide was held to be dishonourable. Norman told me that a young girl had committed suicide and had been buried away from the rest of the village because her death was considered shameful.

Despite their Islamic faith, the villagers brewed potent palm wine in a clearing in the bush. Many of the village men went to this drinking hole and sat sipping the forbidden brew on upturned palm stumps.

Norman and I went to a place called Dhows Inn that served Western food and ate sausages and chips. It was a novelty for me to eat that sort of food, and for Norman too. He mostly ate whatever food was available in the village.

Norman had a little shortwave radio and listened to the BBC World Service on it. I too was a fan. I had been introduced to it by my dad – it was one of his favourite British traditions.

After a couple of days in the village we went to Mombasa. I had told Norman that I had never been to the ocean – it's not the kind of place that's accessible to people on callipers and crutches – and Norman vowed that he was going to find a way to get me there.

We travelled through the bush and suddenly there was an expanse of white coral sand in front of us. The waves were lapping gently against the shore and the palm trees were rustling in the wind. The beauty of it all took my breath away.

Norman had said he was going to take me to the sea and he was the kind of man who stuck to his word. He hired a bicycle, put me on it and pushed me across the sand and right down to the water's edge. When the bike could go no further, he gave me a piggyback right into the water. I couldn't swim, but Norman held me so that

I floated. I loved and trusted him so much that I knew he would keep me safe.

From where I was lying I couldn't see the beginning or the end of the ocean. Feeling the warm water splash over my body was both relaxing and liberating. It felt very therapeutic to immerse my whole body in the sea. I felt weightless, no longer disabled; in fact floating in the water made me feel that I barely had a body at all.

'Oh, Norman,' I said, 'I don't want to ever leave this water. I feel so free in here.'

Norman beamed. He seemed very happy to see me so contented.

'I love you so much,' he said.

'I love you so much too,' I replied. 'I want to be with you forever.'

As we kissed and cuddled with the waves lapping gently over us, I felt that Norman and I were the perfect fit for each other, a two-piece jigsaw encased in the ocean.

It was just before Christmas and we had arranged to visit my family in Nairobi after our trip to Mombasa. Now that I was madly in love with Norman I couldn't wait to introduce him to my family. I was apprehensive about the meeting, though. Some of my family members had never met a white person before.

At first it was a little awkward. 'Why does he look like this?' my relatives kept asking. Some of them were keen to touch Norman's skin and hair, as if he were some sort of museum curiosity. My niece asked if he'd burnt himself to get such pale skin.

I remembered my friend Margaret telling me about when she had travelled to Australia and stayed with a white family who had never seen a black person before. The little girl of the family had said in her presence, 'Mummy, she's so dirty, she needs a wash.'

Fortunately, after my relatives got over the strangeness of Norman's appearance everyone got on well. A goat was slaughtered in Norman's honour. He tried his best to look as if he was enjoying eating it, but I watched the way he chewed it for a long time and seemed reluctant to swallow it. He whispered to me afterwards that it was too greasy for his liking. My sister told me she had cooked it very well because she had heard that Westerners liked to eat very soft foods.

While we were there Norman showed me some of his diary entries since we had met. Looking back over them, it was hard to believe that things had moved so quickly:

Sat. 22nd Aug. The day we met. I'm in love.
Probably she doesn't love me, but I've met a
beautiful girl called Anne Wafula, 28, who's had
polio since she was two and a half and uses
crutches. I plan to visit her in Machakos when I've
finished in Nairobi. I'll phone her from Nairobi
and hope she can tell me if she still feels the same.
She stood in the doorway with crutches and a hat

on and looked absolutely gorgeous. She was so
easy to talk to.

Wed. 9th Sept. Spent 45 minutes on the phone to
Anne. It was really thrilling.

   The headmaster had a phone on the wall. I had
a key to the main school building but not the key
to the phone, which was locked in a box with a
padlock. I discovered a way to climb through the
library and slide my hand into the box, feel dial
the number to Anne and then get the receiver out.

   She said some really nice things and said she
even dreams about me. I really, really want this
relationship to work.

I was very touched by Norman's diary entries. His
enthusiasm for me made my whole body flush with
pleasure. It was already hard to imagine what my life
had been like before he had entered it.

We started making plans for the future. I said that I
would do a master's in Kenya and wouldn't go to
Australia to study after all.

In Nairobi we visited my brother Goddard. He and
his girlfriend Eunice had a baby called Charlene and we
were invited to her first birthday party. We shopped for
some clothes and toys to give her as a present and I
could see that Norman knew how to buy the right
things for children. Charlene was gorgeous and as I
watched how gently and nicely Norman played with her

I thought about what a good father he would make. I longed to have his baby, but remembered with a heavy heart what the doctor had said to me. I sighed and decided that I would have to be the best auntie in the world instead.

Early in 1999 Norman's daughters Jennifer and Sasha came to visit us. They stayed in my house in Machakos for a few days and I took them to Nairobi to meet my family. Sasha was quieter and Jennifer more extrovert, but both of them were nice, laid-back girls and I could see what a good dad Norman was. Like my own dad, he would do anything to make sure his daughters were happy. It was obvious that they all loved each other very much.

By now Norman and I were planning to get married and spend the rest of our lives together. Once it was established that our feelings for each other were mutual it seemed like the logical next step in our relationship.

In September 1999 Norman travelled to my village with me to meet my dad. My dad took to him immediately. He is a good judge of character and was impressed by Norman's kindness and intelligence. He was particularly happy that Norman knew a lot about Kenyan history and about the history of our tribe. He showed him around the farm and pointed out where my mum was buried.

When Norman had a serious talk with him about the two of us getting married, my dad gave his blessing.

Now there was nothing to hold up our plans. My cousin started negotiating a dowry with Norman and said that the family wanted 13 cows in exchange for me.

Norman was shocked. He knew nothing about dowries.

'Don't worry about that, Norman,' I laughed. 'That kind of thing doesn't matter to my dad. He doesn't measure his love for me in how many cows I'm worth!'

We got engaged on 31 December 1999 at the fanciest hotel in Machakos and I had never felt so happy in my entire life. Norman's VSO contract had ended and he was going back to England. He planned to stay there for a while, getting a job as a teacher to save up some money. Now that he had met my family and been approved, I would make a brief visit to England to meet his family and then return to my teaching job in Kenya. When he had saved up enough money he would return to Kenya too and we would have a big wedding and settle down together.

Norman had a friend with multiple sclerosis called Davey who was involved with a branch of the Physically Handicapped Association of Great Britain in the northeast. Norman had told him about me and he invited me to travel to the UK to do a talk about disability in Africa. Everything seemed to be working out very well. I could combine my talk with meeting Norman's family.

I asked for some leave from my college so that I could travel to England. My long-term plan was to get a promotion (I wasn't quite sure how) and become one of the youngest headmistresses in Kenya. My salary would then be enough to support both of us so that Norman would be able to fulfil his dream of writing novels.

Things didn't quite work out like that.

Chapter Eleven

This Green and Pleasant Land

I t was April 2000 and I was beside myself with excitement at the prospect of travelling to the UK, the country my dad held in such high esteem. I saw it as both a land of plenty and the centre of civilisation.

'Take lots of photos that you can show me when you get home,' my dad said to me. I wished Norman and I had enough money to take him with us.

I was terrified at the prospect of flying for the first time and when I saw the aeroplane we were about to get into I wondered how anyone could possibly breathe inside such a small space. Once I got inside, though, I was relieved to see that it looked like a more spacious and comfortable version of a bus. Norman was more scared than I was and confessed that he really hated flying.

Once we were airborne I dreamed of what I would find when we touched down. I had watched soaps like

The Rich Also Cry and *Santa Barbara* on television. These
programmes were set in huge mansions with big swimming pools, fleets of cars and hordes of servants, and I
expected England to be exactly like that.

One of the first things I did see at the airport was two
men kissing. I was shocked, because I had never seen
public displays of affection between two people of the
same sex before. Come to think of it, I had never seen
that sort of thing on *Santa Barbara* or *The Rich Also Cry*
either. What sort of a country had I arrived in? Nobody
was open about homosexuality in Africa and in many
African countries people would be jailed for that sort of
behaviour. I also saw men and women kissing and touching each other's bottoms. I thought that things like that
should only be done in the privacy of the bedroom. I
began to feel uneasy.

We got on a train to travel north to Newcastle.
Norman told me that he wanted to take me to see a very
famous sculpture by Antony Gormley called *Angel of the
North*. The size and beauty of it took my breath away. I'd
never seen anything like that in Kenya.

'There used to be a mine under there and men like me
went underground for generations, digging out coal,'
Norman told me. He explained that the sculpture marked
the transition in the British economy from mining, a
transition Norman himself had experienced.

I never ceased to be impressed by his knowledge. To
me he seemed like a walking encyclopaedia.

Suddenly, without warning, he dropped down on one

knee and, looking very serious, said, 'Anne Wafula, will you marry me?'

I started laughing. 'I've already told you many times that I'm going to marry you, Norman.'

'I know, but this is a very special place and I wanted to hear you say it with the *Angel of the North* as our witness.'

'I love you, Norman,' I said.

Although it was April, it was a cold and windswept day. The chilly temperatures couldn't touch me, though. I felt warm and contented.

I was eager to find out how everything worked in the UK, but a lot of things were very disappointing. For a start, I couldn't see any houses of *Santa Barbara* proportions. In fact I couldn't believe how tiny the houses were – the mud hut I was born in was bigger than some of these uninspiring little boxes.

In Kenya professional people like teachers often saved up their money, bought a piece of land and then built a nice house on it. So everyone's house looked different there, but here all the houses looked the same. That seemed very strange to me.

I was also astounded when I discovered that children often put their elderly parents in institutions. I thought of how I had longed to have my grandmother living with me so that I could look after her in her final years and I found it very difficult to understand why that didn't happen here.

When I went to the supermarket I couldn't believe that you could buy meals that had already been cooked, vegetables that had already been chopped and rice that had already been picked clean of stones. The concept of frozen meat surprised me. I wondered how long ago the animals had been killed. The pre-packed food didn't taste as good as the fresh and simple food I ate back home where people went daily to the market to buy fresh tomatoes and onions, and I missed the simplicity of those things.

Life moved very fast in England and I began to understand why Norman became impatient when he had to wait six hours for a bus to come along.

There were plenty of things that impressed me about England, though – good roads, lush green fields and lots of sheep. I was amazed at the family doctor system and loved the fact that everyone had their own bed. I liked the way the gas for cooking was always there in the kitchen. In Kenya people went to a petrol station and filled a cylinder with gas if they wanted to use it for cooking.

One of the biggest joys was having access to clean water that never stopped running out of the taps. In Kenya there were always water shortages and power cuts. Sometimes we didn't have water because it was being directed to a rich person's farm. A lot of water also went to water the big flower plantations that supplied British and other supermarkets. When I saw British people buying these flowers I said to Norman, 'I wish people could see how ordinary Kenyans have suffered to bring these flowers to the UK.'

I was impressed by all the different channels that were on television and the fact that letters were delivered to people's homes. In Kenya people had a key to a mailbox at a central post office and had to go and collect their mail there. I thought it was the height of luxury and civilisation to have letters brought to your doorstep.

But ... 'Where are the swimming pools in the back gardens?' I asked.

Norman just laughed at me.

I felt very let down.

I was also really shocked when I found out that some people couldn't read and write. The British were the people who had brought literacy to us. How could it be that some of them were illiterate?

I went to church and was surprised to find most of the pews were empty. The British people had brought Christianity to Africa and used religion to govern Kenya. Yet here it seemed that a very small percentage believed in the God they had introduced to us.

Norman wanted to take me to London. He explained that the capital was very different from other parts of the UK. I was excited to see all the famous landmarks like Big Ben, Buckingham Palace and the Tower of London. I was conscious of a lot of people staring at me, though, as I struggled along in my callipers and crutches. There were many differences between England and Kenya, but the staring was a major similarity. As usual I pretended I was unaware of the piercing looks and tried to carry on with the sightseeing.

At a train station an elderly lift operator looked at me and said, 'Why are you walking on those things, love? We haven't used them in this country for more than 50 years.'

'Oh, really?' I said. 'I'm from Kenya and we still use callipers and crutches for people with my kind of disability.'

Over the next few days I looked through the crowds to see if I could see anyone else using callipers and crutches. I saw a few wheelchair users, but it seemed that the lift operator was right – there was no one at all using the heavy contraptions that I dragged myself around with. Norman had mentioned to me that people in England used wheelchairs, but I had told him I was used to my callipers and crutches. In my mind I still thought of wheelchairs as the makeshift taxis that the staff at Joyland used to put a few children into at once rather than a permanent means of getting around.

In Newcastle I met Norman's family – his sisters and brother. It was nice to see his two daughters again as well. All of them were incredibly warm and welcoming to me and accepted me immediately. I had expected it to be hard because I was such an outsider, but all that seemed to matter to Norman's family was that he adored me and that I was making him happy.

I was also pleased to find that after all the time I had spent with Norman I had adjusted to his Geordie accent and didn't have a problem understanding what his family and friends were saying to me.

I met his friend Davey, who had invited me to give a talk to the local PHAB club. In Africa many conditions don't have names and scientific knowledge about them is lacking. Into that vacuum creep superstitions about witchcraft and strange curses. Multiple sclerosis, for example, is attributed to witchcraft because it strikes when people are already adults. I realised that in the West, however, every condition had a name and a rational explanation. I was happy to see that here people knew what conditions they suffered from and how to get the best quality of life they could. People had social workers to support them and social groups to attend where they could meet other people with the same disability as them. Kenya had disability clubs, but everyone was lumped together irrespective of the nature of their disability.

When I gave the talk at the PHAB club in Jarrow, I could see that people were shocked by the circumstances I described.

'It makes us feel very grateful for the kind of support we have here,' said one member of the audience.

A couple of people lifted my crutches and couldn't believe how heavy and cumbersome they were. I didn't

understand why they were making such a fuss. In Kenya
many disabled people crawled on boards with wheels on.
Some were beggars and shook tins at people who drove
past them.

'Surely those are the people they should be feeling
sorry for, not me, a teacher,' I said to myself.

The plan at that point was still that Norman would find
a teaching job in Britain while I returned to Kenya. But
after I'd been in the UK for about a fortnight, he said to
me, 'I can't bear to let you go. I know we agreed to wait
a while before getting married, but the thought of
being parted from you tears me apart. I don't want to
spend even a minute away from you. Let's get married
now. Stay here with me, I'll get a job and then we can
go back to Kenya together when we've saved enough
money.'

This was a major change in our plans, but I was so
much in love with Norman that I agreed immediately.
It's true what they say – love can move mountains. Like
Norman, I felt that being separated by a continent was
more than I could bear. And because of my Christian
faith I wouldn't live with him without being married to
him, so it made sense to get married.

I had come on a visitor's visa, so I knew that I
wouldn't be able to get a job in the UK. I would have to
give in my notice at Machakos and look for a new teaching post when we returned to Kenya.

I thought a lot about the relative benefits of life in the UK and in Kenya. I wished I could take some of the positives from the UK and export them to Kenya. I'd like to take the good roads, running water, piped gas and the NHS system. But I would certainly leave the weather behind. I couldn't get used to the lack of sunshine. In Kenya grey skies pass quickly and the sun always returns, making people more cheerful.

Africa is rich in so many different ways. But our political system lets us down. We are lucky, though, because we know who our neighbours are and we look out for one another. In the UK people are more focused on themselves.

Norman is a great romantic and he wanted us to get married in Gretna Green. I had never heard of it, but he explained it was a special place where lovers got married. We travelled there to see if we could have our wedding ceremony there.

I thought that Gretna Green was a very beautiful place with lots of nice trees and flowers. The chapel was small but beautifully decked out with fresh flowers. We sat in the reception area, waiting to see if it would be possible to get married. But to our disappointment they said that I would need lots of official documents from Kenya before any marriage could go ahead. It would take several months to get all those documents and neither of us wanted to wait that long.

Feeling dejected, we were about to leave when the registrar came out and said there was a couple who had arrived to get married but didn't have any witnesses.

'Would the two of you mind doing the honours?' he asked.

We both agreed, happy to be able to help and glad to be present at a wedding in Gretna Green, even if it couldn't be our own.

Once Norman gets an idea into his head he's determined to see it through. He wrote to a church in Newcastle to ask if we could get married there, but they replied saying they were fully booked for the next few months. Undeterred, he went to the civic centre and miraculously they had a space on 6 May, just a couple of weeks away! To my relief, they didn't require the mountain of documents that we had been asked for in Gretna Green.

My dream had been to have a big wedding in Kenya that I could take lots of time to plan. I wanted to be surrounded by bridesmaids and flower girls. But I accepted that it just wasn't practical and that I needed to make the best of the situation we were in. The main thing was that I was marrying the man I loved. The trimmings really weren't important.

I started shopping for a wedding dress. We hired one with a train that I loved. I was a petite size eight with a 22-inch waist. Everyone commented on how slim I was. Norman's niece Amy was a bridesmaid for us and his best friend Jo was best woman. I had never heard of having a best woman at a wedding before, but Norman was happy with the arrangement and Jo was a lovely, warm woman so I was happy too. Norman's friend Helen, who had also volunteered with VSO in Kenya, was maid of honour.

I had no idea how to organise a wedding in a strange country, but Norman's two sisters Christine and Gillian were very supportive and arranged everything. Without them I don't think the wedding would have happened.

I wasn't able to speak to my dad on the phone at that time, but I wrote to him and explained that there had been a change of plan and I wasn't going to get married in Kenya but in the UK. I thought he would be very upset, but he wrote back and said, 'Anne, you have my blessing.' I was so happy to receive that letter.

In Kenya, Norman had promised my dad that he really loved me and that he would look after me. My dad knew that Norman was a good man and that we were in love, and that was what mattered to him. However, he was keen that I should have a get-out clause if we didn't live happily ever after. 'If it doesn't work out, don't suffer in silence,' he wrote to me. 'All I want is for your life to be happy.'

I found it strange that people asked us to send a list of which presents we wanted. Norman assured me that that was the protocol for British weddings, but I felt uncomfortable about it. In the end we said, 'Just bring us whatever you want.'

Norman went out drinking with his friends the night before the wedding. He told me this was traditional and was called a stag night. He explained that women had an equivalent night out called a hen night. I didn't like the sound of it and stayed in with a friend instead. We ate fried chicken and watched a movie. I adored the dress I was going to wear the following day and I couldn't stop looking at it and touching the lacy fabric.

We ordered a wedding cake with the Union Jack and the Kenyan flag on it to symbolise two different people being joined together. I walked down the aisle in the civic centre hall in my callipers and crutches, my bouquet of flowers hanging from my crutch. I felt ashamed of my old, frequently welded crutches and bought festive white ribbon to cover them up.

I wished that the people who had belittled me from my village, those who had cast us out and told my family to give up on me, could witness this moment of great happiness in my life.

There was nobody to give me away. My brother-in-law Tony was supposed to do the honours, but he didn't arrive until the reception had started, so I walked down the aisle by myself. The one sad part of an otherwise wonderful day was not having my dad to walk me down the aisle. I also wished that my mum was still alive to see this day – the moment that every girl dreams of. But I was so happy to be joining a family that loved and accepted me and didn't question me because of my disability. The warmth of Norman's family helped to make up for the lack of my own on this special day.

Both Norman's parents were dead, but his Aunty Bessie, who was like a second mum to him, was there.

She kept saying over and over again to me, 'You are so beautiful. Where did you get her from, Norman?'

Some of Norman's family are Welsh, and having just about got used to the Geordie accent, it was too much for me to start deciphering another unfamiliar one! Nevertheless, I spent the whole day smiling. I was certain that I had found the love of my life and that the months and years ahead with Norman were going to be full of joy and friendship and laughter as well as passion.

We knew that we were taking on more responsibilities than most newly married couples. Both of us would have to sacrifice part of our culture so that we could meet somewhere in between. We would be starting a new blended culture of our own. It would be a big challenge. We had already argued about certain issues. Norman hadn't been able to understand why my house in Machakos was constantly full of people. The Western culture is not to share your living space in that way. In the West what you have is yours, but in Africa what you have is shared with the community. After a few disagreements Norman did say, however, that he admired our culture of sharing so many things. We both knew that giving things up and meeting in the middle don't just happen overnight, but one thing we promised each other was never to have secrets from each other and never to lie. We were two very different people brought together by love and felt that love really could conquer all.

After the ceremony many of Norman's friends and relatives came up to me to congratulate us and wish us lots of luck for the future. I felt that I was floating somewhere above the ground on this huge wave of goodwill that was directed towards us.

Some of the food at the reception was unrecognisable to me – Norman had to explain what prawns and quiche were. If the wedding had taken place in Kenya, chickens and goats would have been slaughtered. I stuck to familiar foods and didn't want to eat too much in case I got an upset stomach and spoiled things for my honeymoon.

Norman's friends Andy and Helen had kindly offered to drive us to our honeymoon – a caravan park at Haggerston Castle in Northumberland. Davey's wedding present was use of his accessible caravan for a week.

I was very excited about the whole thing. I'd never seen a caravan before apart from on television when I'd watched *Carry On Camping*. Norman explained that they were houses that people sometimes travelled in.

The shower in Davey's caravan was easy to get in and out of and there was a ramp which I referred to as a 'steep slope'. The area was really beautiful, but I didn't get to see too much of it because I couldn't go far on my callipers and crutches, so we spent a lot of time in the caravan talking and watching TV.

Norman often spoke about his two daughters. 'Wouldn't it be fantastic if we could have a child together?' he said.

'I'm so sorry, I don't think I can have kids,' I said sadly. 'I would really love to have a big family, but I've seen different doctors in Kenya and they all said I wouldn't be able to carry a child.'

'It doesn't matter, Anne,' Norman said kindly. 'What will be, will be. Honestly, it makes no difference to me. My happiness is complete knowing that you're my wife.'

'I've wanted a baby for so long,' I confessed. 'Having a baby would make our happiness complete. If we do have one, it will be a gift from God, but if we don't we could adopt one.'

I knew how many children were crying out for love in Kenya and I would have been happy to adopt one, but at the same time I really wanted us to have our own child. Even though I knew that pregnancy was not on the cards, I spent my entire honeymoon longing to be a mum. I kept hoping a miracle would happen. I knew Norman wasn't going to walk away if I didn't get pregnant the way that some men in my country would have done, but it didn't make me ache for a baby any less.

I kept sending silent prayers to God: 'Dear God, if you can just let me be a mother you will remove all my shame about being disabled at a single stroke. I've never wanted wealth or a swimming pool or a car like the people in *Santa Barbara*, I just want You to give me a child so, so much.'

I felt that being able to give birth to a child would make up for all the bad things I'd been through in my life.

* * *

After our honeymoon I resigned from my teaching job in Machakos and concentrated on getting used to life in England.

Norman got a job as an English teacher at a school in Harlow and we moved there in May 2000. He was due to start teaching in September. We had very few possessions between us – just a suitcase and a rucksack. Norman had given all his possessions away before he'd travelled to Kenya to work for VSO and I had left most of mine in Kenya, assuming I'd be returning there very soon.

We found a flat to rent on the eighth floor of a tower block. I'd never seen such a tall building that people lived in. In Nairobi there were tall office blocks, but not houses.

There was a lift, but I disliked the place from the start. It swayed in the wind, which would have been alright on the ground floor, but not on the eighth. When Norman went out to work I felt very lonely and isolated. It was too difficult for me to go out by myself on callipers and crutches, so I became very dependent on him. I was frightened of falling down if he wasn't there. In Kenya I was used to the terrain, but here I wasn't.

We had hardly any furniture and slept on a blow-up mattress. When I was in Kenya I had had a nice bed to sleep in, status in society and a good standard of living. Now I had come to a rich country and was struggling at the bottom of the pile.

Although people worked hard in Kenya, they also knew how to enjoy their leisure time. Here it seemed that all people did was work.

There were some drug dealers living in one of the flats near us. People arrived at all hours of the day or night and used a password to get into the flat. I didn't know much about drugs, but did know that it was easy to get addicted to them. The trail of people knocking at the drug dealer's door looked pale and ill and desperate. To me, their addiction looked like a kind of imprisonment. I decided that given the choice, disability was better than addiction. At least I still had some control over my life.

'I want to go back home. I'm so homesick,' I said to Norman when he came home from work that evening. 'Let's forget about raising the money here and just go back. I belong in Kenya and want to be near my family. I'm so lonely being stuck in the flat by myself all day long when you're at work. If I go back to Kenya I'll be a respected teacher once again and I know my life will be much happier.'

'I'm sorry it's so tough for you, sweetheart,' said Norman, stroking my hair. 'But it will be so much easier for us to go back to Kenya with a bit of money in our pockets. Just try to hang on a little bit longer. I'm sure things are going to change.'

Chapter Twelve

A Miracle

Norman was right. Things were about to change.
As well as feeling lonely I had started feeling ill. Exhaustion and nausea washed over me in horrible waves. I sometimes woke up feeling very dizzy and it took a while for the bedroom to stop spinning around.

'I think I've got malaria, Norman,' I groaned after the fifth successive day of this. 'I know that sometimes people feel very sick and weary in the early stages. Could you go to the shops and get me some malaria tablets?'

'Anne, you're in England now, you can't just buy malaria pills over the counter the way people do in Kenya. Everything is on prescription here. If you have got malaria you might need to go to the Hospital for Tropical Diseases in London for treatment.'

'If I have malaria I want to go back home and die there,' I said.

Norman took my temperature and found it was normal.

'Usually people get a fever with malaria,' he said, 'and you haven't got one. Let's see how you are tomorrow and if you're no better we can go and see the doctor. I think it's a bit premature to talk about going home to die.'

He was trying to make me laugh, but I wasn't in the mood for jokes.

I gazed out of the window at the bricks on the outside of the tower block and longed to bite into them. 'What on earth is the matter with me?' I asked myself. 'I think the malaria is making me hallucinate.'

I was so busy worrying about my mental and physical health that I didn't notice at first that I'd missed my period. When it did register, I wondered if it was due to coming to a strange country and eating unfamiliar food. Then suddenly in a blinding flash I wondered whether I didn't have malaria at all. Could I be pregnant?

I hardly dared believe that it could even be a possibility. I knew what the doctors had said and I told myself to stop being silly. But I couldn't help hoping and dreaming that maybe the miracle I'd prayed for for so long had finally happened. Even hearing the word 'pregnant' inside my head made a big smile spread across my face.

As soon as Norman got home from work I blurted out, 'Can you get me a pregnancy test? I think I could be pregnant because I've missed my period.'

Norman's face lit up, but then logic took over. 'I'll get you one, Anne, but don't get your hopes up. You know what the doctors said.'

The next day he came home from school with a pregnancy test in his bag. I hurried to the toilet, speed read the instructions and did the test. A clear blue line showed in the window of the test, confirming that I was indeed pregnant. My heart pounded with joy.

'Norman, Norman, look, it's positive!' I cried, waving the test at him. 'We're going to have a baby!'

Norman looked disbelievingly at me and then at the test. 'Anne, you know those things sometimes get it wrong. I'll speak to my sister Christine about it. She knows all about this kind of thing.'

He rang her and asked if these tests were often inaccurate.

'You fool!' she cried. '*Of course* she's pregnant. You need to get her to the doctor right away.'

At the GP's surgery my doctor, Dr Ogbonnaya, did another pregnancy test.

'It's positive!' she said, grinning.

I screamed with joy and kept saying over and over again, 'Thank you, God, thank you, God. You heard my prayers.'

Then I burst into tears.

'I've waited for this moment for so long,' I said. 'The doctors in Kenya told me it wouldn't be possible for me to bear a child. I need to pinch myself to make sure I'm not dreaming.'

The doctor was very interested in my pregnancy because of the polio, a condition she had rarely encountered. She said that I would need to be monitored by a consultant obstetrician throughout my pregnancy, rather than mostly by a midwife, as was the case for women with straightforward pregnancies.

A few days later the morning sickness started in earnest. And when the initial excitement had subsided I remembered what had happened to Grace and suddenly felt scared. But I didn't tell Norman because I didn't want to alarm him.

I wrote to my dad to tell him the good news. He wrote back and said he was overjoyed and was praying for us every minute.

'The Lord is blessing you. May you continue to be blessed,' he said.

By the time I was two-and-a-half months pregnant I was experiencing extreme discomfort. I felt as if something was tearing my stomach apart. I went back to the GP and explained to her how I was feeling. She examined me and said that I must start using a wheelchair because the pressure of the growing baby on my pelvis could put both the baby and me in danger. It had never occurred to me that continuing to walk on my crutches and callipers could be so risky. It was the only way I knew of getting around.

I was given a wheelchair a few weeks later. That day my life changed forever. I couldn't believe how easy everything became when I could wheel myself around and was no longer dragging myself forwards with the help of heavy metal and cumbersome leather straps. Before I was permanently exhausted; now I had energy to do other things.

It was as if I had been reborn. I could transfer myself from bed to wheelchair without help from Norman. It gave me an incredible sense of freedom and independence.

Although I sighed with relief when I discarded my callipers and crutches, I did also feel some regret. I had always had a love-hate relationship with them. They had been as much a part of me as my withered legs since I was four years old. They had caused me a great deal of pain and discomfort, but I respected them because they had got me to a lot of places and allowed me to do a lot of things that I wouldn't otherwise have been able to do.

My body felt so light without the metal and leather encumbrances. But sometimes I put my polio boots and callipers on just to remind myself of how things used to be. I couldn't stand up in them anymore because of my pregnancy, but I knew that for as long as I lived I would never forget them.

The day I got my wheelchair Norman and I went shopping in town to celebrate my new-found liberty. I received far fewer stares in my chair than I had when I was walking around in my callipers and crutches – antique pieces of equipment, I now realised, by British standards.

For some disabled people, especially those who have previously been able-bodied, a wheelchair underlines their difference from others and makes them feel stigmatised. It reminds them of what they've lost. But for me the wheelchair made me feel much closer to the able-bodied world than callipers and crutches ever did.

One of the pleasures of the wheelchair was that I could hold Norman's hand as we moved along the street, something that had never been possible when I was struggling along on callipers and crutches. He was used to being constantly on standby in case I fell, but now that I was in my wheelchair he could relax. My regular tumbles were consigned to the past. And there were no more sore thumbs, fingers or elbows for me.

Now that I no longer had to stand, all the pressure was taken away from my hips and thighs and I didn't have to wear my ugly polio boots.

'Norman,' I said, as we passed a shoe shop, 'I want to buy myself a pair of high-heeled shoes, something I've always dreamed of wearing, and a pair of trainers for comfort. I know I won't be able to walk in them, but I just want the pleasure of seeing something pretty on my feet.'

'You can buy as many pairs of shoes as you like, sweetheart,' said Norman indulgently. He took pleasure in my childlike delight at my changed circumstances.

I bought a pair of black shiny stilettos. It was difficult to get them on, because my feet faced in different directions and were different sizes. The stilettos didn't look good on me, but I really didn't care. Now I could say truthfully that at least once in my life I had fulfilled my ambition of wearing high heels.

When we got home I asked Norman to take pictures of me in my new shoes and send them to my dad and my sisters. Even though I looked weird in the pictures, I wanted everyone in Kenya to see that it was possible for a woman living with limbs ravaged by polio to wear pretty shoes.

Although I celebrated the fact that I was going to have a baby every minute of every day, I spent a lot of time worrying about all the things that could go wrong. Every time I went to the hospital to see my consultant I held my breath in case he delivered some bad news about the baby. However hard I tried, I couldn't get Grace out of my mind.

I also continued to feel very sick and struggled to keep food down.

One day I got a call from my doctor. 'Hello, Anne, it's the GP here. Don't panic, but can you get a small bag and get down to the hospital now? You are extremely anaemic and need a blood transfusion urgently.'

'Oh no, is it going to harm the baby?' I cried.

'No, don't worry. The transfusion will boost your iron levels and then you'll feel much better. It should stop that dizzy, lightheaded feeling you've been having,' she said.

I had thought that the dizziness was a normal part of pregnancy and was delighted that something could be done to sort it out.

At the hospital I was given three units of blood and was put onto strong iron supplements. As my GP had promised, I did start to feel a bit stronger after that.

I missed Kenya and my family so much during my pregnancy. Had I been at home, all my extended family and friends would have fussed around me, making sure that I had everything I needed.

When Norman and I went into town I grinned broadly whenever I saw another black person, hoping against hope that they too would be Kenyan or, even better, from my village. That would be the next best thing to having my family around me.

I started approaching people and saying, 'Excuse me, are you from Kenya?'

Norman was concerned. 'Anne, you can't keep going up to every black person in town and asking that question,' he said. 'They might take offence. A lot of people in Harlow are of Caribbean origin, not African. They might find it a bit odd if you keep asking them whether or not they're Kenyan.'

One of the teachers at Norman's school *was* Kenyan, however, and she came to visit me during my pregnancy bearing gifts of flour, bananas and green vegetables. I was so excited to have access to almost African food.

The doctors and the midwife said there was a risk that the baby might have certain disabilities and I panicked.

Did they know something they weren't telling me? They assured me that they hadn't seen anything worrying on the scans, but wanted to do an amniotic fluid test, a procedure that increased the risk of miscarriage, just to be sure.

Norman and I discussed it and decided not to go ahead with it.

'However this child comes out, we will give it the best and love it,' he said.

I thought of how my parents loved me just as much after I contracted polio as they did before.

'A child is a blessing whether or not it has a disability,' I said. 'If we aborted an imperfect child, how would we know whether or not that child might be the one destined to discover a major cure for cancer? I grew up in Africa where it was so difficult to be disabled. Why wouldn't I bring up a disabled child in a Western country where there is so much more support for people with "imperfect" bodies or minds?'

My feelings of nausea continued. I hated the smell of onions and any kind of soap. When Norman started cooking his dinner, I urged him to put wet towels under the kitchen door to hold the cooking smells in and to open the windows. Even then the smells crept into my nostrils, so finally I begged him to eat before he came home. All I could face eating myself was bland, boring porridge and tinned pineapple.

A few months before the baby was due we moved from the tower block to a bungalow, which made life a lot easier for me.

As the pregnancy progressed, both Norman and I got more and more excited. I overheard him talking to his friend once saying, 'Old Normie is going to be a daddy.'

I was convinced that I was going to give birth to a boy and had recurrent dreams in which I was holding a baby boy. We decided that if it was a boy we would call him Timothy after Norman's great grandfather.

Norman's daughter Jennifer came to visit us and every time the baby started kicking she put her hand on my stomach and said, 'Timothy is kicking, how sweet.' She too was convinced that the baby was going to be a boy.

Because I didn't have stomach muscles, the baby slid from side to side. Sometimes my bump looked normal and sat in the centre of my abdomen but then suddenly it would lurch to one side, making me look very peculiar.

The consultant obstetrician was very interested in my case because he had never had a polio pregnancy before. He was keen to use me to teach medical students. I had mixed feelings about the extra medical attention. It was nice to be so well looked after but it made me more aware of all the things that could go wrong. There weren't many moments during the pregnancy when I wasn't anxious.

My hormones were very erratic, too, and poor Norman bore the brunt of my black moods. One night when I was seven months pregnant, in a fit of pique over something trivial I packed my suitcase and declared that I'd had enough of England and was returning to Kenya.

Norman managed to calm me down before I disappeared off into the night in my wheelchair.

The doctors told me that it wouldn't be possible for me to have a normal delivery and prepared me for an elective Caesarean a few weeks before my due date.

On the appointed date Norman and I arrived at the hospital trembling with excitement. I couldn't believe that we were about to become parents. The pregnancy had felt interminable and hadn't been easy, but it was all worth it now we were about to hold our precious baby in our arms.

I was taken down to the operating theatre, had various tubes inserted into my hand and was about to be put on the operating table when a nurse came rushing in saying that there was an emergency case of a baby with a cord wrapped around its neck and would we mind waiting until the following day? Of course we agreed, although we couldn't help feeling a strong sense of anticlimax, especially as it was 8 February, Norman's late father's birthday.

When we went into the operating theatre the next day the staff had prepared one cot with a blue blanket and one with a pink one.

'No, we'll only need the blue one,' I said. I was so certain that I was about to give birth to a boy.

This time there were no last-minute upheavals. A light blue sheet was put up in front of us so that neither of us could see the incision being made in my abdomen. But I could see in silhouette surgical implements being passed from medical hand to medical hand. All I could feel when the baby was pulled out was a sensation of pressure leaving me. Norman held my hand and suddenly we heard the sweetest sound of a baby being slapped and crying.

'It's a boy!' said the doctor beaming.

'I know,' I said, tears of joy rolling down my cheeks.

The nurse put him on my chest. As soon as I felt my baby's skin against mine I started sobbing uncontrollably. I never thought I'd experience this moment that other women took for granted. Norman was crying, too, and so were some of the medical team. Through my tears I gazed at the perfect, tiny creature that I had grown inside me despite my useless stomach muscles and powerless legs. How had this happened? It could only be down to a miracle.

'Hello, Timothy,' I said through my tears.

He weighed seven pounds, which amazed the medical staff because I had had such a difficult pregnancy. A lot of babies also come out looking like wrinkled old men, but he was a smooth and perfect little creature. I felt very proud.

After all the years of wishing and longing, I was a mum at last. I imagined how sweet it would be if I had my mum and grandmother by my side to share this moment with me. They had accompanied me on the journey through the early years of my life and they would understand better than anyone what this meant to me.

Norman wished that his mother could have been there too to see him cut the cord.

The million anxieties I had had during the pregnancy vanished instantly. Timothy was perfect and seemed to grow more beautiful every time I looked at him. At that moment I was the happiest person who ever lived.

Norman too kept looking at Timothy. 'What's wrong with the baby?' he demanded.

I started panicking. What on earth was he talking about? The hospital staff had said that Timothy was a fine healthy baby.

'What do you mean?' they said.

'He's white,' Norman cried. 'He should be brown.'

'Don't worry,' the midwife reassured him. 'His skin will darken, you wait and see.'

As I lay exhausted in my hospital bed a few hours later I overheard one of the nurses saying to a midwife, her voice choked with emotion, 'Who said that it couldn't be done?'

I glowed when I heard her say that.

I'd thought it was going to be so easy to look after a baby, but I soon realised it was going to be more difficult than I had anticipated. I struggled at first to do anything at all for Timothy. I was in agony because of the

Caesarean wound and all I could do was lie on my back and let the nurses do everything for me.

Whenever Timothy cried, I had to ring the bell and call the nurses. But I felt guilty that they were doing the things for my son that I should have been doing. Although it was illogical, I even began to feel jealous of them because they could do things for my baby that I couldn't do myself.

It was hard for me to breastfeed and Timothy was so greedy that I was feeding round the clock, so I was constantly exhausted, but at the same time I was cherishing every moment.

When Timothy started expelling greenish black meconium, though, I panicked.

'Don't worry, Anne, this is normal,' the midwife said reassuringly.

Some of the staff were very good and helped me to try different ways to look after Timothy. By a process of trial and error I worked out the best ways to be a disabled mum.

When I got back home with Timothy, the idea of leaving him in his cot went out of the window. It was so much easier for me to have him in the bed with me so I could feed him and change his nappy easily. Baby textbooks were all very well, but they didn't fit in with real life, not my real life anyway.

One of the things that did work well was putting Timothy in a sling and then wheeling myself around the house.

Norman helped with the washing, cooking and shopping, and I tried to sleep when Timothy was sleeping. I really wished I had my family around me, though. It would have made all the difference in the world during those early months.

Norman went to school early in the morning and when he came back in the evening he started on all the household jobs, so he too was exhausted. He helped me to do the bottles, because I was supplementing breast milk with bottles. Although he was constantly tired, he said that having Timothy made him feel young again. He had still been a teenager when his older daughter had been born and he was enjoying being a parent again from an older, wiser perspective.

Timothy's weight dropped a little after the birth and once again I panicked, not realising that this was normal. The doctors were worried that I wasn't feeding him properly, but he soon began to gain weight. He developed some blueish marks on his body, a development that alarmed me, as they looked like bruises. But I was told it was a condition sometimes found in mixed-race babies called Mongolian blue spots. After a while the spots faded away.

I felt that at first there was some scepticism about my ability to care for my baby because of my disability. I was asked to keep a chart of everything I was doing for Timothy. But thankfully the health professionals soon saw that I was a capable and devoted mum and that my precious baby was thriving.

We sent my dad lots of gorgeous pictures of Timothy from every possible angle. People called him 'thunder thighs', because he had meaty thighs. According to my dad, mine had been exactly the same.

Although my disability meant that it was impossible for me to carry Timothy on my back in the African way, I was determined to experience the feeling of having my baby nestling against my spine, even if it was just for a few moments, so Norman placed him on my back as I sat in my wheelchair and helped me to tie him to me in the traditional way. As I felt his warmth against me, I couldn't stop smiling. Now I could say that I had carried my son on my back in the same way that my sisters carried their children and my mother had carried me. I was very happy that Timothy had tasted his Kenyan origins.

When Timothy's eyes started to focus we gazed at each other for hours.

'What a beauty you are,' I kept saying to him.

When he started crawling, he followed me everywhere. He was so fast that he sometimes ended up under my wheelchair. Once he followed me to the toilet and then promptly fell asleep under my wheelchair. I was stuck. I couldn't get out of my wheelchair to pick him up and I couldn't move my wheels in case I crushed him. Fortunately after about ten minutes I heard Norman's key in the door.

'What on earth are you doing, Anne?' he asked.

'Shhh, Timothy's sleeping,' I whispered.

Norman realised what had happened and crawled under the wheelchair to pick him up.

Like me, Timothy walked at nine months and again like me he started making sounds at a very early age.

I was too young to remember my able-bodied self and watching Timothy gave me the strangest sensation. It was like watching and remembering my younger self from a different body. As I watched him take his first sturdy steps, I thought of my own first steps. It made me long to be able to walk so that I could rise up from a chair like any other mum and swing him around, or pick him up when he stretched out his arms to me. When he did that, Norman had to pick him up and put him in my arms. But although I felt my loss of mobility acutely when I watched Timothy, it also made me feel good to relive my young, healthy self through my son. It was like recapturing an important lost memory, a missing piece of myself.

I kept pestering my local surgery about Timothy's vaccinations. I wanted to make sure that he was immunised against polio at the earliest possible opportunity. I asked so many times that I'm sure the staff got quite irritated by me. When he finally was immunised against polio I made the nurse double and triple check the batch date on the vaccine to make sure it was not out of date and was the right strength and quality.

'I understand why you're anxious,' she said to me, 'but please don't worry. The vaccine is good quality and Timothy will be as fully protected against polio as every other child who receives it.'

I nodded, but couldn't help worrying that something might go wrong. After all, I'd been immunised and still got polio.

Timothy ran almost as soon as he could walk and when we went out we had to put him in reins to prevent him from hurling himself headlong into oncoming traffic. I sent a picture of him in reins to my dad and he wrote back horrified and said, 'Why are you chaining your child like a dog?' I tried to explain about roads and traffic and danger, but my dad didn't understand and accused me of torturing my child.

When Timothy was coming up to his first birthday he managed to open the front door, because we had very low door handles, and ran outside. My heart was racing as I followed him in my wheelchair. But the faster I pursued him, the faster he ran. He thought it was a wonderful game. I called out to a passing woman to grab him before he got to the road, and fortunately she did. After that we realised we needed some extra help.

The council provided us with a part-time carer. She pushed Timothy's buggy and I pushed myself alongside them in my wheelchair. It made things so much easier.

I was determined not to let the carer take over, though. I wanted to be 100 per cent mother to my baby. When we went out shopping with Norman, people stared because I pushed Timothy's buggy while I sat in my wheelchair and Norman pushed the wheelchair. We called it our special train. We were such a happy family.

Having my own flesh and blood gave me more joy than I will ever be able to describe.

As a toddler Timothy loved playing football. I often went into the garden with him and he would move my leg to make it kick then run to the other side of the garden, kick the ball back to me and say, 'Kick now!' I would throw the ball back to him and he would say, 'No, kick it, Mummy, kick it!'

He didn't understand that I had a disability. Sometimes he wanted me to sit in his buggy so he could sit in my wheelchair, which he considered to be superior.

When he started to understand that the wheelchair was something I needed, however, he became very protective of it. If anyone went near it he pushed them away and said, 'For Mummy.'

Sometimes when we went into town and Timothy saw another person in a wheelchair he looked at me to make sure I was still in mine. He couldn't understand that there could be more than one person in the world in a wheelchair, because he thought it was something unique to his mummy.

When he passed the age of two and a half and continued to grow and develop I was overjoyed that he was so healthy and active, but I shed a few quiet tears because in him I saw what I could have become if polio hadn't stopped me in my tracks.

Chapter Thirteen

Getting the Fitness Bug

Having a child changed everything. Suddenly it didn't seem so easy to go back to Kenya after a year or two, as we had planned. It was very expensive raising Timothy and we realised it would take longer than we had envisaged to save enough money to return. We decided to put the plans on hold, although it remained our dream to return at some stage.

I had applied to do a master's degree in educational psychology at Cambridge and had been accepted. The course appealed to me and Cambridge was within manageable commuting distance of Harlow. I had assumed that I would be able to combine my studies with being a mum, but hadn't anticipated just how exhausted I would feel and also how difficult I would find it to be parted from Timothy. I explained to the university that I wouldn't be able to take the place after all.

Almost by accident I fell into something completely different. A friend of Norman's called Barbara often took photos of me.

'You have a strong, attractive face, Anne, and more importantly, you're very photogenic,' she said. 'You should give modelling a try.'

I was flattered and remembered the photographer who had approached me in Kenya, but I didn't do anything about it.

A couple of months later we were approached in town by a couple of people offering us cards for different modelling agencies. It triggered my interest and a few months later we contacted a reputable agency called Visible People. The director, Louise Dyson, said she would take me on her books.

The agency started putting quite a bit of work my way. Some of it was campaigns for improved rights for people with disabilities and some of it was general modelling work, including brochures for companies. It made me feel good to be photographed alongside women who were considered beautiful. Theirs was a very different kind of beauty from what was regarded as beautiful among the women in my tribe – the markings scored into the skin.

I enjoyed promoting the disability rights messages as well as having my photo taken. I was amazed when my face was plastered across billboards in London as part of a campaign by the Disability Rights Commission. The slogan next to my photo said, 'I'll never get a seat on the board, I'm in the wrong chair.' I felt very proud to be part of something that was trying to change stereotypical attitudes towards disability. There was nothing like this in Kenya and I felt happy that in the UK disability issues were taken more seriously.

At one point I was offered a large sum of money to feature in disabled pornography. Needless to say, I declined. As a mum and a Christian, the idea of destroying my reputation and my dignity in that way was completely out of the question.

I had been a size eight for most of my adult life, but to my horror I had crept up to a size fourteen after Timothy was born. I had developed a taste for takeaways and used to ask Norman to bring fast food home for me. I'm sure that my family in Kenya would have been appalled to know how I was eating. They always prepared delicious healthy food from scratch.

Now my clothes felt tight on me and I could grab handfuls of flesh across my stomach, something I had never been able to do before. It was hard to believe that I had been one of the skinniest girls in my primary and my secondary schools. I had also probably put on weight because I now spent so much time sitting in my wheelchair. Before, using my upper body to swing myself forwards on my crutches and callipers had acted as a perpetual workout for me and had made my arms and chest very strong and toned. Now that my crutches and callipers lay unused in my cupboard, those muscles had turned to flab.

'I don't like being the way I am,' I said to Norman. 'I want to go back to being a petite girl again. I much prefer myself that way. What can I do about it?'

'I love you whatever size or shape you are, Anne,' he replied, 'but if you do want to lose a bit of weight, why not go down to the local gym and see if they can help you with some exercises for your upper body?'

My knowledge of what happened at gyms was very hazy. I remembered the big empty hall at Joyland with mats in it where we lay down to have our physiotherapy. But I was sure that English gyms were very different.

When I arrived at my local gym, I explained that I was wheelchair-bound as a result of contracting polio as a child.

The instructor who was showing me round scratched his head. 'That's not a condition we're used to working with here. I suggest you go to your GP and ask for a referral for a specific exercise programme that would be achievable with your disability and then we'll try to put something together for you.'

I returned to my GP and she provided a letter of referral for me. I had no idea that in England doctors could give people a prescription to go to the gym.

Unfortunately, the machines in the gym weren't wheelchair-friendly. 'Hmm, we'll have to be a bit creative here,' said the instructor.

All of the staff were encouraging and did their best to help. I started working with one of the instructors, a man called John Campbell, who was a former British body-builder. He helped me to sit on various different machines, including a stationary spinning bike, and anchored me with his heavy body-building belt.

'Your upper body strength is excellent,' he said as he watched me exercising. 'Are you sure you've never been to a gym before?'

I explained about the callipers and crutches.

'Oh, I see,' said John. 'Well, I'd like to do some cardio work with you to strengthen your lungs. There's an outdoor track here and you can try to do a lap of it in your wheelchair and see how you get on.'

That seemed a daunting prospect to me, but I managed to push myself round at what felt like a snail's pace. Then I spent the next ten minutes trying to get my breath back.

Thanks to John, my fitness did increase, however, and to my delight I started losing weight. The exercise also boosted my self-esteem and made me feel happier and more settled in England.

John explained to me that there were lots of opportunities to get involved in wheelchair sport if I was interested: 'There's wheelchair javelin, wheelchair basketball, wheelchair racing, all kinds of things ...'

I looked at him open-mouthed. I was aware of the existence of visually impaired runners, but had no idea that disabled sport went beyond that. Most of my life had been focused on struggling to move my body from one place to another without falling over or collapsing in an exhausted heap. But now that I was in a wheelchair perhaps I could start using my body in a completely different way. If I wasn't pouring every last ounce of strength into keeping myself upright I could concentrate on trying to do some good things with the part of my body that did work well. My brain started fizzing with possibilities.

'If you're interested, I know that the track at Harlow Running Club is also used for disabled sports,' said John. 'Why don't you go along and find out what's on offer there?'

Now that I'd tasted exercise I was keen to see where it might lead me. I went to Harlow Running Club and met the club secretary, Terry Martin, and a coach called Alan Stevens. One of the club's disabled athletes was Noel Thatcher, a visually impaired 5,000 and 10,000-metre runner who was ranked very highly. I also met a disabled woman called Isabel Newstead, who was a pistol shooter and had won a lot of medals.

Terry and Alan started to talk to me about wheelchair racing and suggested that I had a go at it. I didn't even know what it was, so they had to start from scratch and explain all the basics to me.

I watched wheelchair racers on television competing in the 2002 Commonwealth Games in Manchester and felt excited and impressed by their speed and fitness. I felt as if a whole new world of possibilities was opening up to me.

There was one racer, an Australian woman called Louise Sauvage, who really impressed me. Her upper body strength was incredible. I'd never seen anything like it before. 'That is a true sportswoman,' I said. The way she pushed her racing chair was so impressive. Her determination shone through and the amount of power that she transferred from her body to the chair absolutely fascinated me.

To begin with, Terry made me go round and round the track in my wheelchair. Proper disabled wheelchair racers had special racing chairs that looked a bit like elongated tricycles, but I never imagined that I'd get to the stage of sitting in one of them and was content just to be getting round the track in my ordinary wheelchair.

It was so exhilarating to speed along as fast as my arms could turn the wheels of my chair and I loved the feeling of the wind on my face. I felt that this was the closest I'd ever get to running.

Many disabled athletes in the UK have had time to try out a variety of different sports in order to find the one that suits them best. But I'd left it very late before doing anything at all. I was already 30 and decided that if I was going to pursue any sport I might as well stick with wheelchair racing.

I started seeing Terry twice a week. He encouraged me to build up my speeds as I did laps around the running track, but it never occurred to me to take up the sport competitively. It was simply a hobby that I enjoyed, something that got me out of the house and helped me lose weight.

'It would make so much difference if you could get a proper racing chair,' Terry said.

'I'm happy in the chair I've got,' I replied, thinking that what I'd never had I wouldn't miss.

But Terry was determined that I should have the opportunity to use something better than my ordinary wheelchair. He approached the Harlow Recreation Trust and asked for funding for a racing wheelchair for me. To my delight, they agreed to buy me one in May 2002, made to measure by a specialist company.

I had always been the girl who did something else when my peers got involved in sport – at Kereri I had played the piano or read my Bible. Spectator sports had never interested me and instead I'd chosen to watch soaps, films and fashion programmes. Sport had never been a part of my life on any level and now here I was in possession of a shiny new racing wheelchair, getting interested in something that until recently I hadn't even known existed. A new and unexpected opportunity had come my way and I was determined not to let it slip away.

The first time I sat in my racing chair I didn't know what to do with it. I tried to turn it around the way I turned my ordinary wheelchair around and ended up in a heap with the chair overturning and landing on top of me.

'This isn't like your day chair,' said Terry. He didn't know anything about wheelchair racing, though, and had to go and do some research so that he could advise me how best to use it. However, what he lacked in knowledge, he made up for with enthusiasm.

'I'm not an expert, Anne, but I really think you've got potential,' he said.

His words were the sweetest music to me.

Terry continued to train me and people started to complement me on my beautiful shoulders and toned muscles. One able-bodied female friend said to me, 'Anne, I've been working out in the gym for six months and haven't managed to look as sleek and toned as you do.'

Once I got the hang of my new chair, I started to build up speed in it. I felt the same rush of adrenaline as I whizzed round the track as I imagined a Formula One racer felt.

On racing chairs there are small wheels on top of the big wheels, known as push rims, that you push to make the wheels turn. I felt so free when I was pushing them. Every time I sat in my racing chair and pushed I thought of my disabled friends in Africa. I wished they could have the same chance that I was getting. I knew that some of the children I'd been at Joyland with had grown into stigmatised adults, able to do nothing more than sell sweets on the streets. Many were exploited and didn't know where their next meal was coming from. But I was embarking on a new journey, one I never thought would be an option for me.

* * *

Terry was desperate for me to enter my first track competition. I'd already entered two 10K road races at Silverstone and Thruxton and had completed the Silverstone event in 40 minutes, which was very respectable for a first attempt. Other women in my category were finishing in 30 or 32 minutes. For me it was thrilling enough just to be on the start line and the finish line. I wished that my dad had been there to greet me on the finishing line of my first ever race.

In the beginning I wasn't interested in winning; the sheer excitement of taking part was enough for me. I watched the other women with admiration and wondered if I'd ever be able to push like them.

Still, I could now travel faster than I'd ever been able to go in my entire life. As a person who had never been able to keep up with my peers when they strolled down the street, I found the ability to go so fast was beyond thrilling.

My training programme was fairly haphazard because I had no idea what sort of a plan the top wheelchair athletes were following. I worked with Terry twice a week and went to the gym once a week to do cardio-vascular work.

The first track event that Terry entered me for was the Eastern Region Championships Disability Sports. I couldn't believe it when I won five gold medals.

Then he entered me in the British Wheelchair Championships at Stoke Mandeville. I came first in the 100, 200, 800 and 1500 metres and second in the 400 metres. As I hit the finishing line pure euphoria surged through me.

I hugged and kissed Norman afterwards.

'What you just did is absolutely amazing,' he said.

'I'm so, so happy,' I told him. 'I can't believe I've won medals.'

These events were a real turning point for me. I had tasted winning and although I had a long way to go I had got a glimpse of the kind of athletic success I had never dreamed it was possible for me to achieve. I vowed to train harder so that I could improve at my sport.

Norman was incredibly supportive. I devoted myself to Timothy during the day when he was working and then went to train in the evenings when he got home from work. Although I was developing a passion for wheelchair racing, my family was my biggest priority and I didn't want anything to get in the way of that. Racing was a temporary thing, but being a mum was for life.

I entered the Disability Sport England Championship, an international event. It was here that I was classified for the first time. There are different categories of classification for disabled athletes according to the severity of the disability. This is to try and make things as fair as possible and to ensure that athletes are competing with people with the same level of disability as them. It's quite a technical process.

The assessors looked at the way I pushed on the track, then physiotherapists examined me and asked me whether I could stand up and walk. I explained that I used to use callipers and crutches, but couldn't walk unaided. I described my crutches — the kind that fitted under the armpits rather than those that looped around the wrists. They asked me to perform certain exercises, such as sit-ups. I was unable to do them because of my disability. They also asked me to kick my legs, but since I'd had polio my legs had never worked at all.

In disabled athletics the categories for wheelchair users range from T51 to T54. T51 is the least able and T54 the most able. Some cerebral palsy sufferers who can walk also do wheelchair racing. They are classified separately. After my assessment I was classified as a T53. I didn't really understand what that meant — I was just grateful to have a chance to compete.

Once I started taking part in races, my mind and body switched to a different mode — I became competitive. I had been competitive in my studies in Kenya and now I wanted to be the best I could be in this sport.

Soon after the Disability Sport England event, though, my racing chair was stolen. I used to leave it locked in a cupboard at Harlow running track along with a chair belonging to a young boy who was also doing wheelchair racing, and both chairs were stolen. Terry was furious and I was absolutely devastated. I'd hardly got started and now someone had pulled the rug from under my feet. Getting involved in racing had really boosted my self-esteem. Losing my chair felt as if someone had chopped off my arms.

Terry told one of the DJs at the local radio station what had happened and he agreed to launch an on-air campaign to raise money for a new racing chair for me. I was overjoyed. My faith in human nature was restored when I saw that so many people were prepared to help me by contributing to a fund for a new chair for me.

We had planned a family visit to Kenya for August 2003 and I was thrilled when two days before we were due to leave, the radio station told me they'd paid for my new chair and it was now ready for collection from the manufacturers. I'd be able to take it with me to Kenya. I couldn't have left England a happier woman.

Chapter Fourteen

Going Home

We had wanted to take Timothy to Kenya as soon as he was born, but balked at bombarding his little body with too many vaccinations. When he was two and a half, we felt he was old enough to travel to the country of my birth. I was dying for my beautiful little boy to meet all my family and get acquainted with his Kenyan roots.

Various family members had hired a *matatu*, a minibus, to come and welcome us at the airport in Nairobi. The reunion was a joyful one for me. I had forgotten just how much I missed my country and my family.

Timothy seemed to know instinctively who his family was. My sisters' and brothers' little girls, Sandra, Charlene, Sonia and Natasha, were standing on one side of a glass partition where family and friends waited for their relatives to emerge after they had passed through customs. The five children started playing a silent game lining their palms up against one another's, even though

the glass divide prevented them from physically touching one another.

The lift at the airport wasn't working, so I had to take
a long route round the airport to reach my family. I had
got used to everything working in England and had
forgotten how things were in Kenya. 'Oh, I'm home,' I
said to myself.

The welcoming party consisted of about 50 people –
immediate and extended family. Everybody made a big
fuss of Timothy. I felt so proud of him as family member
after family member scooped him up for kisses and
cuddles. He took the whole thing in his stride and
seemed to be enjoying all the attention that was being
lavished on him.

The plan was to travel in the minibus to the village,
where my dad and the rest of the family were waiting for
us. After three years in England, the number of potholes
in the Nairobi roads really struck me. Before, I had never
noticed the state of the roads because I had nothing to
compare them with. But I loved the friendliness of the
people. Everyone we met was so welcoming and seemed
to enjoy a much simpler life than the one I had got used
to in England.

It took us the whole day to travel to the village. We
saw many wonders along the way that made for a
dramatic contrast with Timothy's life in Harlow – herds
of sleek zebra and groups of playful baboons.

'Stripey horses, stripey horses,' he said, clapping his
hands in delight. We stopped so that he could feed them.

There's a place on the way to my village that is directly on the equator. It's a big tourist attraction because you can put one foot on one side of the equator and the other on the other. People love having their photos taken with a foot in both halves of the world. It was very emotional for me to be there because the last time I'd visited and straddled both sides of the world I'd had no idea that the next time I did this I'd be blessed with a child.

The atmosphere in this place that runs along the centre of the world is strange – there is a difference in air quality on the two sides. Standing on one side is like standing in the sun; standing on the other side feels more like standing in the shade.

When we arrived at the village I saw lots of familiar faces as well as some absences. Some people had died, while others I remembered as young girls and boys had married and had children. The generations were moving steadily along the conveyor belt of life.

Reassuringly, my dad looked exactly the same. I was so happy to see him. He had been prepared to risk his position in the village to protect and defend me and had sacrificed so much for me. I felt that my love for him was overflowing from my body. Now it was my chance to make him feel proud of his daughter.

Many villagers came to meet my new family and me, and my dad welcomed them all. He had assembled all the elders to greet us. We all sat under a big shady tree while he and the others drank the Jameson whiskey that we had bought duty-free.

'This is the real stuff,' my dad beamed.

A year before I had started buying new clothes and bags as gifts for my family and extended family. When I handed out the presents everyone seemed delighted with them – it was like a day at the 'go down' market in Webuye without people having to rummage around.

The village looked much poorer to me than before, because now I was comparing it with England. Yet it struck me how happy people seemed, even though they had so few material possessions. They walked barefoot, but showered us with traditional gifts like vegetables and millet flour. Everything they had they were willing to share. Kenya is very far from perfect, but this was a quality I really missed. In the West there is much more emphasis on the individual and what that person can achieve. Here people worked together as part of a community. In the West people owned more things but were often less happy than the people I saw around me now. 'What is the true route to happiness?' I wondered.

So many different emotions surged through me as I sat in the village I'd been born in. I was very happy to be returning to my roots. Yet I had left the village as someone who had been despised by part of the community. My whole family had been stigmatised here as a result of my illness, but now I'd come back as someone who had succeeded in education and, more importantly to the villagers, succeeded as a woman because I had borne a child.

I had long hair extensions, which people had never seen before. They didn't realise my luxuriant locks weren't my own hair.

'It must be all the different foods you eat in Europe,' said one teenage girl who couldn't take her eyes off my hairdo.

They were also fascinated by my wheelchair, a piece of equipment they had never seen before.

'You're so lucky to have your own little car, Anne,' they said.

The news had spread that I was back in town and people walked for miles just to see if it could really be true that that crippled girl who had been driven out of the village now had a child.

Some of the older people kept looking from me to Norman and then to Timothy before finally pronouncing, with the authority of doctors who have just carried out a DNA test, 'Yes, this boy is really your child.'

The women were eager to know the details of how I'd managed to give birth with a disability like mine.

'How was childbirth for you?' they asked, gathering around me.

They wanted to see my scar. Not many women in the village had had a Caesarean. Really the only option there was to give birth naturally, even though some women died in the process. I showed them my small scar and explained that the doctors had removed the baby while I was awake.

'Those white people, the things they do,' the women kept saying, shaking their heads.

My sister and sister-in-law both lived in Nairobi, so they had access to Caesareans at the local hospitals, and they both had a big vertical scar from the breast to the groin from their first child. At the second birth the doctors had cut them horizontally so they both had a big ugly cross-shaped scar emblazoned across them, and they envied my small neat scar.

The women were also intrigued by the fact that Timothy was mixed race. They had never seen such a child before and wanted to touch his hair all the time and look into his eyes. They marvelled at how beautiful he was.

One of the old women came up to me and said, 'Anne, if you have made it this far, only a fool would say there's no God. He has been looking after you to get you where you are now.'

One of the traditions of my tribe is that little boys select a goat which is slaughtered in honour of their birth. My dad asked Timothy to pick out a goat he liked. He wasn't sure how to respond to the goat he chose and tried to sit on it like as horse. In keeping with the custom, though, he held the tail while it was slaughtered. He didn't flinch at all, probably because he was too young to realise that the goat was about to lose its life.

'Oh, this is a real Bukusu warrior,' the old men cried, impressed that he was not afraid of holding the goat's tail.

Then the goat was roasted and Timothy was given a particular rib to eat, in keeping with tradition. Norman was too squeamish to watch the slaughter, but out of respect for my family he ate the meat.

My dad laid on a big spread for us – goat, chickens and traditional brew for the elders. My step-mum Florence had prepared special food for a son-in-law, a porridge made of millet and sorghum which Norman declared was delicious. Special milk was prepared in a gourd and mixed with the ash of certain herbs.

Norman tried to greet some of my female relatives by hugging them, but they took fright and ran away, because in our tradition there should be no physical contact between a son-in-law and his wife's step-mother and aunties. I had to explain the cultural mores of our tribe to Norman. He apologised profusely when he realised he'd unintentionally made a faux pas.

Over the next few days more than 80 people came to visit us and check us out. The villagers who had once said that I was bringing bad luck to the community were now giving us gifts.

It seemed that my illness had helped to change attitudes in the village. My dad told me that when people were struck down with unidentifiable illnesses now they said, 'We can't give up on them. Look what happened to Anne.'

What happened to me was making me quite anxious about Timothy. I was delighted to have him in Kenya, but every time he cried I checked him over carefully, terrified that he had contracted polio.

I shared my concerns with Norman and he did his best to reassure me.

'Timothy has received good-quality immunisation against polio and various other conditions. Nothing bad is going to happen to him. Just try and relax,' he said.

We decided that we would set up a library in the village, which we would stock with educational books and books for pleasure from both Kenya and England. As well as furthering people's education I hoped that having access to a range of books would broaden their views of the world. I made a mental note to send over some Mills & Boons.

I sat with my aunties and other women from the village and helped them to peel potatoes and bananas. I felt so proud that I was accepted as one of them.

My dad proudly showed Norman what he was growing on his farm. His sugarcane crop was thriving and Norman was very impressed. It was the best feeling in the world for me to see the two of them together. Even though Norman had come from a different world, my dad and the villagers welcomed him just like any other son-in-law who was valued in the community.

Some of the very old people, like my 90-year-old great-aunt, had never seen a white person before. Her sight was fading and she pulled Norman close so that she could get a good look at him.

'Do white people pass wind and go to the toilet?' she asked, wide-eyed.

My sisters and I couldn't help laughing. 'Of course they do,' we replied, conveniently forgetting what we ourselves had thought as children.

Everyone was fascinated by how white people lived, but even those who could speak a bit of English couldn't understand a word Norman said.

'Tell him to speak more slowly,' they cried.

Some of my female cousins asked me if I could find them a white husband. But others weren't so keen.

'I'd be so scared to sleep in the same bed with a white man,' some of them whispered.

When it was time to leave the village I had tears in my eyes. I knew that some of the people who were waving and wishing us good luck didn't know where their next meal was coming from. It felt strange to know that I'd soon be returning to a life where all our food was bought from a supermarket where I could choose from ten different kinds of beans. I wondered what the villagers would make of frozen meat on a polystyrene tray. I asked myself if I was going back to happiness or leaving happiness behind me. To this day I have never satisfactorily answered that question. Having one foot on one continent and the other foot on another can be quite disorienting.

After we left the village we travelled back to Nairobi and then to Mombasa to have a holiday by the coast. Nairobi to Mombasa is called one of the great train journeys of the world. However, it passes through a big slum in Nairobi. While we were there, children ran up to the train windows begging for sweets or money. It was evening and the slum dwellers were preparing to settle down for the night in their makeshift homes of cardboard boxes, paper and corrugated iron.

I looked at the slum children scampering around and then at Timothy and it completely broke my heart.

'There's no justice in the world,' I said to Norman with tears in my eyes. I wished I could mother all of those children.

I had taught Timothy to say 'Jambo', the Swahili word of greeting, and he kept saying it to the slum children who were waving to him through the train window. They were begging him to take off his clothes and give them to them. Of course he didn't understand a word they said and just kept on waving and smiling.

It distressed me that there were so many people suffering one way or another in Kenya. As I looked out of the train window, lush fields and small villages flashed past. I knew that there were people in some of those villages who had similar disabilities to me, people who were ostracised, had no resources and spent their lives crawling on their hands and knees.

When they served dinner on the train, I couldn't bring myself to eat. I looked at Timothy's little hands as he clambered all over me. They were so soft and innocent. I imagined how the hands of the street children the same age as Timothy would already have roughened because of the harsh life they were leading.

The next morning we arrived in Mombasa. The smell of sea and seaweed filled our nostrils and lifted my spirits. The ocean was sparkling blue-green and palm trees offered lots of shade. Timothy whooped with joy when he saw the sea.

There is a Swahili proverb, 'Going to the coast is like going to a wedding and leaving and going back to the village is like going to a funeral.'

Norman showed Timothy where he had lived when he was teaching. His former students were all very keen to see the 'half-white, half-black child' that Norman and I had produced.

We rented a modest apartment at Diani Beach for a holiday with my brother, my older sister, my two sister-in-laws and their families, who lived in Nairobi. It had no running water in the bathroom, so my sisters had to carry water for me to wash with. It did have a flush toilet, though.

Timothy kept saying, 'Mummy, beach. Mummy, beach.' He loved it so much and would have been happy to stay forever. He picked up some Swahili from his little cousins and learned enough to communicate with them. He adored spending time with them.

Monkeys would come and snatch our food when we were eating and Timothy found that hilarious. He loved the sea so much that it was a fight to get him back to the house. I went into the ocean with him. To be floating in the beautiful clear water with my precious boy in my arms was the most wonderful feeling in the world.

We relaxed completely and didn't have a care in the world. In this little corner of paradise none of the concerns of the outside world could intrude.

We visited Machakos during our trip so we could show Timothy where his parents had met. There was a school for people with disabilities there and I had sometimes visited the children there when I was teaching at the technical college. The head teacher saw me as a role model for the children. I had given talks to the children and encouraged them to achieve in life. Since we had been in England we had been regularly sending money to the school. Davey had done a 24-hour fast to raise money for the children and Norman had put a jar on his desk and collected small change from his pupils. It had soon mounted up and we had sent it to help pay for the renovation of the school's toilets and showers and to buy new mattresses and blankets. We also bought the school a special cooker so that the pupils could eat soft maize and beans. It was wonderful to visit and see that the quality of the children's lives had improved as a result of our fundraising.

My family gave us a farewell party in Nairobi. Another goat was slaughtered, adding to the toll of animals who had lost their lives in our honour.

My dad rarely got drunk, but he became quite merry and talkative at that party. 'If any of my daughters wants to marry a man from a different culture,' he said, 'I give my blessing as long as the man has integrity, because I can see how happy my daughter and Norman are together.'

I felt so proud that my dad had given my marriage to Norman such a resounding seal of approval.

Some of my friends came along to the farewell party. It was great to see them again. They were amazed that I had had a child, and such a healthy one.

Every second of my trip I was filled with happiness. I didn't want any of it to end. As we travelled back to England I thought once again about how blessed and privileged we were. I felt very sad to be leaving Kenya and my family, but I was returning to England refreshed and invigorated and was determined to redouble my efforts to succeed at wheelchair racing.

When I got home I spoke to Terry, my trainer. He told me that the radio station that had raised the money for my new racing chair wanted to present it formally to me in October. I was delighted that I would have a proper opportunity to thank everyone who had contriuted to the purchase of my new chair.

Terry moved away from Harlow after that and Alan Stevens took over as my coach. He was also coaching Noel Thatcher, the visually impaired runner who had won several medals. Noel was preparing to represent Great Britain in the 2004 Paralympics in Athens. Everyone was working hard to try to get good enough times to qualify.

I attended some of the British championships and did well in some of them. After one race one of the British officials said, 'Your pushing is getting much better, Anne. Will you be representing Kenya in the Paralympics in Athens?'

The idea thrilled me. I had spoken to some Kenyan Paralympic officials when I was in Nairobi and they had asked me to put my racing chair through its paces in Kasarani stadium as they were not familiar with wheelchair racing. Kenya was renowned for its excellent visually impaired runners and for its wheelchair throwers, but it didn't have any wheelchair racers. The officials had said they would consider me if I got good racing times at the beginning of 2004.

'I've spoken to some of the Kenyan Paralympic officials about it and they say it's a possibility if my times are good enough,' I replied.

It was surreal that I, Anne Wafula, the girl from Mihuu village in western Kenya, could even contemplate taking part in the Paralympics. But maybe it wasn't such a ridiculous notion after all. I was determined to do everything I could to get to Athens.

Chapter Fifteen

Athens

I got in touch with the Kenyan officials who were
working with the country's Paralympic athletes, but
the person I spoke to didn't seem to know anything
about my visit to Kasarani stadium.

'I'm a Kenyan wheelchair racer living in the UK,' I
explained. 'I've made good times in my races and have
won a few gold medals in UK competitions. I'd love to be
a part of the Kenyan team going to Athens if you're
prepared to consider including me.'

The voice at the other end of the phone sounded very
sceptical. 'Kenyans don't do wheelchair racing,' he said
matter of factly.

'Well, I'm Kenyan and I'm doing it,' I replied.

He asked what my times were and when I told him he
sounded slightly more interested in me.

'OK, if you want to try to get onto the team you'll
have to come to Kenya to qualify.'

'Will I be racing against anyone?' I asked.

'Just the clock.'

So in August 2004, with a free flight courtesy of Kenya Airways, I arrived in Nairobi. My brothers and sisters came to greet me at the airport. It was wonderful to see them, but I couldn't spend much time with them because I had to go straight to the Olympic training camp where both able-bodied and disabled members of the team were staying.

After a few days of training I did timed trials by myself. I qualified and they put me in the team.

I was delighted, but being so new to wheelchair racing, and indeed to any sport at all, I don't think I realised at the time quite how big a deal it was to be competing in Athens at the Paralympics.

Paul Tergat, one of the fastest marathon runners in the world at the time, was very kind and friendly towards me and was very interested in my racing chair.

'We have seen these bicycles when we are running and they are really fast,' he said, sounding impressed. 'It's so good to see our own sister having a go at it.'

My training was a bit of a struggle because the knowledge of my Kenyan trainers about wheelchair racing was extremely limited. They entered me for the 400, 800 and 1500 metres, assuming that like most Kenyan athletes I would be better competing in the middle-distance events. In fact I was stronger at the shorter sprints, but the officials were reluctant even to enter me for the 400 metres. 'That is too short a distance for a Kenyan,' they said.

But then they looked at my times in my category, compared me with others in the world and said, 'Actually, you could do well in sprints. We'll move you into the sprinting category when we get to Athens.'

Preparing to leave Kenya and go to Athens was so exciting. The able-bodied Olympics was first, so the athletes competing there went ahead of us and we watched their performances on television. Some of the people I'd sat and eaten dinner with at the training camp did well at Athens. I was so excited for them and the fact that they had won medals gave the rest of us a big boost. We were determined to do as well as them.

Going to Athens was particularly symbolic for me because of my middle name.

'It's as though God told me to give you that name, Anne,' my dad said to me. 'Go and enjoy Greece and make sure you visit Mount Olympus.'

'I'll try, Dad, if I've got time,' I laughed.

Some of the disabled athletes had been to the previous Paralympics, but others were also participating for the very first time. I was carried along on a wave of excitement and felt as if I was living in a blissful dreamland. Just four years before I hadn't even known that the Paralympics existed and now here I was flying into Athens to compete in it.

On our way to Greece we stopped over in Egypt for a night. We were booked into a very expensive hotel and some of my female teammates who had not left Kenya before didn't know what to do with some of the things in the rooms. I had to explain to them what a bidet was and that if they drank anything from the fridge they would have to pay for it. One of the girls said she was frightened because she might not be able to make her bed properly in the morning, so she just slept on top of it for fear of messing it up. Everyone marvelled at how big and clean the rooms were. But they were not impressed by how small the portions of food were.

I had studied Egyptian history at school and I was thrilled when we were told we were going to see the pyramids. Unfortunately, we had to look at them through the bus window. Because of our disabilities, they decided not to take us off the bus.

When we arrived in Greece we were taken to a training camp to acclimatise. Although we were all used to heat in Kenya, the heat there is dry. In Athens it was very humid and I found it hard to adjust. The moist air made my body feel very heavy and it was more exhausting to move around.

The Greek national football team were also staying at the training camp, along with teams from New Zealand and the United Arab Emirates. One of the men from the UAE, a thrower, sat outside every evening singing beautiful songs and banging a small drum. He became the unofficial camp entertainment.

For the first time I got to see many disabled sports I had no idea existed. There was shooting, archery and weight-lifting. I kept saying 'Wow,' every time I saw something that I'd never seen before. Although I was very grateful to be competing at all, I wished I had discovered disabled sport as a teenager so that I could have tried out a few different activities to find out which suited me best.

More than 90 per cent of the athletes had either had accidents or suffered from spina bifida or cerebral palsy. I was desperately looking for other polio survivors, as I was hoping to compare notes about common problems and training techniques particularly suited to my condition. I did find some competitors from Mexico and Thailand who had had polio, but sadly we couldn't communicate with each other because we didn't have a common language.

A few days before the competition started we moved to the Paralympic village, which was marked by an avenue of flags representing all the countries taking part. The accommodation was accessible, with ramps and other adaptations. In this global village of disability, sport had brought us all together to achieve one common goal. I was so grateful to the person who started the Paralympics off – Sir Ludwig Guttmann, a German Jewish refugee who became the first director of the spinal injuries unit at Stoke Mandeville. He saw sport as part of the healing process and had left us a wonderful legacy.

In the village I met so many heroes and heroines from all over the world. One woman had no arms. She picked up her purse with her legs, unzipped it with her feet and took money out to make a phone call. I felt very inspired by her. In Kenya a woman like that would have been as good as dead. I later found out that her sport was dressage. 'How on earth does she get on a horse?' I wondered. She told me she was disappointed because her horse wasn't well and couldn't recognise her. I imagined how close their relationship was and could understand how disappointed she felt.

I felt relatively able-bodied next to her and it made me feel extremely humble. I felt that irrespective of how well I did, I was taking part in something historic.

I met two lovely supportive wheelchair athletes from America, Jessica Galli and Cheri Blauwet. They had been racing for several years and were excited to see that a woman from an African country was getting involved.

'It would be fantastic if you could win a medal and get onto the rostrum,' Cheri said.

Their encouragement and generosity of spirit gave me a huge boost. Sadly, it turned out to be too late for me to enter the 100-metre sprint, so I went ahead with the races the Kenyan officials had entered me for. I took being entered in the wrong events not as a drawback but as a challenge. I was really excited to be there and knew how much it would mean to disabled people in Kenya because this was a new sport for the country.

Norman and Timothy came out to Athens for two weeks to cheer me on. I was very happy to see them, but couldn't spend as much time with them as I would have liked because there was so much going on.

I'd never seen an opening ceremony on television and I didn't know what to expect. I felt very excited and was determined to enjoy every second. The Kenyan officials had given us traditional African outfits to wear for this big event.

'You're representing not only your own country but the whole continent and you need to look the part,' they said.

A fleet of buses arrived in the Paralympic village to take us to the stadium. When we arrived the place was packed out. I trembled with excitement. 'It doesn't get better than this,' I thought to myself. 'How amazing that I am part of this extraordinary event.'

Timothy and Norman had VIP seats and Norman was snapping away like a paid-up member of the paparazzi. The atmosphere was so highly charged with emotion that I couldn't stop the tears from rolling down my cheeks. I saw a few others dabbing their eyes too.

The whole stadium went dark then was flooded with lights. The focal point was a huge tree in the middle of the stadium. Singers and dancers entertained everyone with traditional Greek performances.

Norman told me afterwards that he swelled with pride when the six of us in the Kenyan team came out in wheelchairs with the others limping behind. Seeing so many disabled people from all over the world, a couple of people behind one flag for the smaller countries and hundreds from places like Great Britain and Canada, was very powerful. In total, 135 nations were competing. I really felt that sport had the ability to unite nations.

As the different athletes marched into the stadium, the Paralympic spirit of encouraging people to participate irrespective of their disabilities shone through clearly. I was trying to stay composed, but I wanted to shout from the rooftops, 'I'm here, I'm competing in the Paralympics!'

I had never in my life experienced anything like it. I wished so much that my dad and my mum could have been there, along with all the other people who had supported me on my journey. I also wished that all the disabled people selling sweets on the streets of Nairobi could have attended. I was sure it would have lifted their spirits so much.

'How come I didn't know that this wonderful event existed?' I asked myself. This wasn't the world of disability I knew. Here we were all different but all equal and all on the world stage together. Surges of joy like bolts of electricity shot through my soul.

Even though Timothy was just three years old he managed to stay awake until the end of the ceremony, which went on until late in the evening. He didn't understand everything that was going on, but he knew that this was something very important for his mummy. Afterwards he kept saying excitedly, 'Oh, Mummy, I saw you. Did you see this? Did you see that?'

It meant so much to me that my husband and son were there to share this special event with me.

When I started competing in the races the atmosphere was absolutely electrifying and I was on fire with excitement.

My first race was the 800 metres and it showed that I lacked both skill and fitness. As I got near the finishing line, Timothy, who was sitting near the front, cried out, 'Go, Mummy, go!' He didn't understand how the competition worked and thought that I was the winner, even though I crossed the line last.

I wasn't too disappointed, though, because I was still learning. Some people there had been training for years, but I had only started training seriously in October 2003, so there was still plenty of time for me to improve. Also, I knew that I had been blessed with a strong upper body and arms. As a child, I had had a very strong grip. My dad said that if I hadn't been disabled, I would have been very tall and strong, with the walk of an elephant.

Though I had finished last, I felt a huge rush of adrenaline simply because I had taken part in the race and made history as the first wheelchair racer from Kenya. I hoped that others would be encouraged to get involved too. Footage was screened in my country and people were more interested in the fact that someone from Kenya was taking part than in my position in the race.

The one race I did do well in was the 400 metres. My time in the qualifying heat was good enough for me to go through to the finals. When I looked on the board at the end of the race, there was a 'Q' next to my name for 'qualified'. I was thrilled.

When they called out 'Anne Wafula from Kenya' at the start of the finals, the crowd cheered. They knew that I was the first Kenyan and in fact the first East African to participate in this sport, and they wanted to do their best to encourage me.

When the starting gun went I wasn't as fast as I should have been because I was concentrating too much on enjoying the moment. Although I came last again, I was delighted because I'd had a go. To those who hadn't believed in me I said silently, 'Look at me now,' and to those who had believed in me I said, 'Thank you for helping me to get here.'

One of the visually impaired runners from Kenya had won two gold medals and broken a world record. Kenyans were very proud of him. They were also very supportive of me. Qualifying for the finals in a sport that Kenya hadn't been involved in before was big news. My sisters watched the reports of my success on the television and called me to tell me how proud they were of me. My dad had a colour television in the village and all the villagers gathered to watch me on the flickering screen. He told me that when I crossed the line they all stood up and cheered. They couldn't stop talking about this strange kind of 'bike' I was racing in.

In the Paralympic village every time someone came back with a medal everyone cheered. Although I didn't have a medal around my neck, I hoped I had done Kenya proud and other disabled people proud. Everyone talks of medals, but only three are awarded in each race and those who haven't won them have also achieved. In my own way I felt that I was a winner. How many people get to go to Paralympics and have their child cheering them on from the sidelines?

I became friendly with lots of other athletes and because I was enjoying the whole Paralympic experience so much I never stopped smiling. One of the journalists reporting on the event for the official newspaper of the Paralympic village, *Pulse*, dubbed me 'Miss Popularity' of the Paralympic village. I felt very flattered and was sorry when the event drew to a close.

The closing ceremony was a similar extravaganza to the opening one, but unfortunately we heard the very sad news that some of the children who were due to attend it had been killed in a bus crash on the way to the stadium. For me, the Paralympics in Athens was something that brought joy to my life, but I knew that for the families who had lost their children this event would be forever associated with grief.

Afterwards I returned to Kenya for a couple of weeks with the rest of the team. At the airport we were all given a bouquet of beautiful roses. Some people extended their hands and said, 'Give us money.' They wrongly assumed we were rich because we were on television. I kept throwing roses out to people as I didn't have any money, and ended up with just one rose left. But I was happy because I felt I was sharing my joy.

I was honoured with a certificate and some prize money for being the first ever East African to compete in the Paralympics in wheelchair racing. Kenyans still didn't know much about the sport – they called it 'bicycle riding for the disabled' – but the fact that I had got into the finals in one race meant that people started to know who I was. They wondered how I would cope with a 'white person's sport'.

Competing in the Paralympics had given me a whole new perspective on wheelchair racing. For the first time I realised that if I focused more and improved my training programme, I could be very good. I learned from some of the other athletes in the Paralympic village that their training regime was completely different from mine. They had been training for much longer than me and they gave me hope that if I trained longer and harder I could reach their standard. For the first time I started thinking of myself as an elite athlete. I liked the sound of those two words as I rolled them around my tongue. 'Athlete' and 'polio' were two words that never used to appear in the same sentence. Suddenly I felt that anything was possible.

When I'd first arrived in England my self-esteem had plummeted. I hadn't been able to get around on my callipers and crutches and I'd felt as if I'd gone back to square one. My pregnancy and Timothy's birth had given me a huge boost, and getting involved in wheelchair racing really had helped me to rediscover myself. When I'd first done a good time, I'd felt that I could fly.

The feeling of the wind rushing past my ears had been exquisite.

I desperately wanted people with disabilities in Kenya to experience the same boost. I gave a talk to a group of disabled people in Nairobi and a few of them showed a real interest in getting involved in the sport.

They also bombarded me with questions about every aspect of my life, from athletics to sex and childbirth. There was very little information available about all aspects of disability in Kenya.

'I try to take each day as a new event and not let what happened yesterday cloud what might happen today or tomorrow,' I said to them.

While I was in Nairobi one of my former primary school friends came to see me and told me that another of our friends was in jail because he had been stealing. I gave her the equivalent of £50 in Kenyan shillings to get him out of jail and met up with him after his release.

'Thank you so much, you're a life saver,' he said. 'You don't understand how hard it is just to survive from one day to the next. Sometimes I have to do bad things to feed myself.'

My friend had got involved with a gang of thieves and been caught by the police – he hadn't been able to run away the way his able-bodied friends had. Once again I realised how lucky I was. Things could so easily have turned out badly for me.

I hoped that while I was in Kenya I could lobby the government and try to encourage them to promote wheelchair racing. Although the country lacked the facilities to develop the sport, there was certainly no shortage of disabled people who could benefit from taking part. I knew, though, that without government support the cost of getting involved would be prohibitive for ordinary Kenyans. A racing wheelchair was the same price as a car in Kenya.

The Kenyan team had a meeting with government ministers to try to encourage them to promote Paralympic sport and spirit.

After that, the government encouraged disabled people to take part in wheelchairs in a marathon for able-bodied people. It was a start and it made me very happy that other people were getting a chance to try out an activity that had changed my life and brought me so much pleasure.

I had missed Norman and Timothy desperately while I had been away and had been racked with guilt about leaving Timothy for so long. The Kenya–Athens–Kenya trip had kept me away from them for ten weeks, the longest we'd ever been apart. Even though I'd seen them briefly in Athens, it just wasn't enough.

'Oh my goodness, I'm missing my child growing up,' I said to myself. I had been there when he had taken his first steps and said his first words. I didn't want to think about all the things I was missing in his development.

'Timothy is fine,' Norman reassured me when we spoke on the phone. 'He's telling all the children at nursery that his mummy is away "winning in Athens". Going to the Paralympics has been the opportunity of a lifetime for you, Anne. You'd never have forgiven yourself if you'd turned it down.'

When I arrived back at Heathrow, Norman and Timothy were waiting to greet me. I covered them both in kisses. It felt so good to be back with my family.

Timothy promptly sat in my racing chair and refused to budge. He kept saying, 'Go, Timmy. Go, Timmy.' I let him play in it for a while because it was a way for him to feel involved in what I'd been doing.

Norman knew all about winning and losing in sport because he was a football fan. He said, 'I still love you, sweetheart, whether you've got a medal or not.'

Timothy chipped in, 'I still love you, Mummy, whether you've got a medal or not.'

Norman and I burst out laughing.

I hadn't won any races in Athens, but nonetheless I returned to Harlow floating on a cloud of euphoria.

Chapter Sixteen

Medals

I couldn't wait to discuss with Alan Stevens some of the tips I'd picked up from the other athletes in Athens.

'Talking to the others and seeing the way they perform has made me realise that I need to work harder and in a different way if I really want to achieve in this sport,' I said to him.

I knew that I needed to spend more time in the chair if I wanted to improve my technique and times, and Alan was happy to help me try to move up to the next level. Together we came up with a much tougher programme and I threw my heart and soul into my training.

I trained about four times a week, but began working at a much greater intensity than before. My training was a mix of pushing the chair more and doing more cardio work at the gym. Although it was gruelling, I was happy that my regime had become much more geared up to the sport that I had fallen in love with.

I kept in contact with Cheri Blauwet, the wheelchair racer I had met in Athens. She was a woman with an extremely good heart. She had won many medals, but to her the sport wasn't just about that. She firmly believed that everyone deserved a chance. We talked a lot about how we could use sport to empower disabled people in Africa.

Cheri was so encouraging to me. Just being in her company made me feel good. Her journey had been very different from mine – growing up disabled in America and growing up disabled in Africa are not the same – but both of us realised what a powerful force for good, sport could be.

'We can use sport to change people's attitudes towards disability,' we kept saying.

People had already started noticing who I was as a result of the publicity I had received in Athens and I received invites to functions in Harlow where I was introduced as a Paralympian. It meant such a lot to me.

I won Kenyan sports personality of the year, which was a real honour, and started giving talks to local people with disabilities about what sport could do for them. I also managed to persuade the local authority to start an initiative to back disabled sport.

Some of the girls in Athens had talked about different makes of chairs, the benefits of different sitting positions and the merits of different sizes of push rim. These were all new things to me. Alan and I experimented with various techniques, learning as we went along by a process of trial and error.

Sometimes he would stand on the track in the freezing cold for an hour and a half coaching me and other wheelchair athletes. He was extremely dedicated and really wanted us to do well.

After a while the new training programme started to pay off. 'Anne, you've moved to a different level now,' Alan said. 'I'm really delighted with your progress.'

In May 2005 I was chosen to represent Kenya in the first ever Paralympic World Cup, which was held in Manchester. It was the biggest international annual multi-sports competition outside the Paralympic Games.

Once again I got a huge buzz from competing with elite athletes and marvelled at the way the atmosphere could be supportive and competitive at the same time. I was delighted to come fourth in the 400 metres and fifth in the 100 metres, competing as usual in the T53 class.

Mingling with the best of the best made me realise just how much more work I needed to do if I was to reach my potential. Even though Norman was earning enough as a teacher to support us, wheelchair racing was an expensive sport and the top Paralympic athletes received some funding, but I wasn't being funded by anyone. It was a Catch-22 situation: to get good enough times to make it into the world rankings you needed to take part in a lot of competitions. But without funding it was hard to get to the competitions.

Racing chairs wear out quite quickly and are very expensive to replace, so I was very grateful when two friends of mine called Stella and George raised money for a new chair for me through a get-together with some friends.

When the 7/7/05 terrorist attacks happened in London I was worried that there might be a backlash against foreigners, especially non-white ones. I had leave to remain in the UK, but I was not a British citizen. The thought that I might be removed from the UK and separated from my husband and son terrified me. I was proud to be Kenyan, but at the same time I loved Britain, was very grateful for all the opportunities it had offered me and regarded it as my home. I thought that if I became a British citizen our family would be more secure, so I submitted my application for citizenship.

It all went through smoothly and I was invited to a naturalisation ceremony with the Lord Lieutenant of Essex. I felt very proud when I became a British citizen and used the naturalisation certificate to apply for a British passport.

I had met a woman called Charmaine at Stoke Mandeville. She supported disabled athletes and I often sought her advice.

'How do I find out about competing for Great Britain?' I asked. She suggested some British officials for me to approach.

I asked the Kenyan Paralympic Association to release me so that I could try to join the British team. I felt bad about leaving them, but the officials were very understanding and knew I was doing it for family reasons rather than because I wanted to desert Kenya.

'Don't forget us. We wish you good luck for the future,' they said.

I contacted UK Athletics and asked if they would have me on the British squad. I showed them my letter from the Kenyans releasing me from their squad and a record of my times. Thankfully, the times were good enough and I was invited to join the squad.

Brian Scobie, one of the top long-distance coaches, was in charge of disability sport at the time and welcomed me to the squad. I also spoke to the British Paralympic Association and expressed interest in competing for Great Britain. The International Paralympic Committee cleared me to switch from Kenya to Great Britain. A new chapter in my racing career had begun.

Soon after I became British, Brian Scobie became my coach. I was delighted because he was highly regarded and very experienced.

I was invited to a training weekend in Sheffield. I had raced against some members of the British team in Athens and smaller events, but hadn't really spoken to them. It felt strange being part of a squad whose athletes

I'd previously competed against. Would I be accepted? How would they look at me? Would they be able to understand my accent? I felt very apprehensive and unconfident. I really wanted to fit in with the British team, but at the same time I didn't want to let go of distinguishing features like my accent, which was part of my identity. I also knew the British team was strong and wondered if I would make the grade.

Norman went with me on the train up to Sheffield. My youngest brother was staying with us for a while and he looked after Timothy for the weekend. I unloaded all my anxieties onto Norman on the journey.

'Don't worry, just take it bit by bit,' he said, as supportive and encouraging as ever.

We arrived at a nice hotel and I met the rest of the team over dinner. Not everyone was friendly, but I thought it only natural that people would be cautious about a newcomer, especially one who until recently had been representing a different country. I felt 'new', which was not a particularly nice feeling.

The next day the people in charge wanted to know what my training programme was. I told them what I was doing and they made some sensible suggestions about changes I should make to my regime in the gym and on the track. They added some specific strength and conditioning components to my schedule.

I was very impressed by the standard of the other athletes and the quality of their training. Their strength and professionalism excited me. Unlike the Kenyans, the

British had a lot of knowledge about wheelchair racing. I felt that here I could really go a long way.

I knew that being part of the British squad would mean being away from home more. Once again Norman was very supportive, understanding that if I wanted to compete at a higher level I would have to make some sacrifices.

'If we can afford it, all three of us will go to events, but if we can't and if it's in school time, Timmy and I will stay behind,' he said.

Everyone in the British squad had light, modern chairs but I had a very old-fashioned one which set me apart from the rest of the team. I realised it was going to take me time to fit in, but I hoped it would happen naturally.

The routines at the training weekends were very different from what I had been used to. Everything I learned I brought back to Alan Stevens to work with at Harlow. Each time I attended a training weekend I learned more and more. I also discovered more about nutrition and the importance of eating a balanced diet while I was training.

After a while I got a more modern wheelchair with orange tyres and a picture of a tiger on the wheels. It still wasn't as up-to-date as some, but Timothy loved it, especially the tiger pictures. Whenever I collected him from school he would jump up and down and say, 'Oh, there's my mummy in her tiger wheelchair.'

The first time I showed up in the playground in it, his friends came up to get a good look at it. 'How come your mummy isn't in a wheelchair?' Timothy said to them. As far as he was concerned, being in a wheelchair was the norm for mums. And all the coolest mums had wheelchairs with tiger pictures. I loved that wheelchair because he loved it.

The Paralympic World Cup took place in Manchester in May 2006. It was strange to be staying in the same hotel I'd stayed in the year before when I'd been representing the Kenyan team. I chatted to some of the disabled Kenyan runners. I was racing for Britain, but would feel an affinity with the country of my birth for the rest of my life, even though I felt British too.

I was extremely nervous, but very excited at the same time. I always looked at what the sport was doing for me as a person, rather than as something that paid my rent and bills. I had started from zero with wheelchair racing. I'd never seen anyone like me doing it when I was growing up, so I had no role models. I was proud of many things I had done in my life – getting a good education, becoming a teacher and being a wife and mother – but this was a different kind of achievement. Wheelchair racing wasn't going to make me rich or famous and I had got into it by chance, but it had enriched my life beyond measure.

When I came down to breakfast on the first day of the event in my red, white and blue uniform, some members of the British team said, 'Oh, those colours really suit you.'

I smiled shyly and said, 'Oh, thank you.'

I felt it was a vote of confidence in me and it really meant a lot to me to hear that.

The Kenyan team members hugged me and said, 'You look fantastic in those colours. We're sure you'll be fantastic on the track.'

Their kind words gave me peace of mind. I was so happy that they bore me no grudge for becoming British.

Prince Edward and his wife Sophie attended the event. Both of them chatted to me and were relaxed and friendly.

Prince Edward said to me, 'I have always loved Kenya and so does my mother, the queen.'

I couldn't believe that I was shaking hands with a prince and chatting to him as if he was a friend I'd bumped into in the street. It all felt very surreal.

Sophie told me she liked my braids and that she enjoyed watching Paralympic sport.

I was dying to tell people back in my village that I'd just shaken hands with an English prince and that his wife had complimented me on my hairdo.

I was racing with British athletes who had achieved a lot. I felt that I could do well, because in training my times were improving. The track was very wet because it had rained just before the race, but I wasn't too worried. I'd never competed in wet conditions before, but I'd pumped my tyres up hard and thought this would help me cope with the slippery conditions. I didn't know that I should have *lowered* my tyre pressures to deal with the wetness of the track. Nobody had explained to me that tyres should only be pumped up to 80–85 per cent of their capacity in these circumstances.

Unwittingly, I'd ruined things for myself. I was taken by surprise when my chair started sliding all over the place. I frantically tried to steer to stay in a straight line but didn't manage it. My chair was aquaplaning. I was the last person to cross the line and was absolutely devastated. I felt as if all the oxygen had left my body. This had been my big chance and I knew I'd blown it.

Nobody else's chair had slithered all over the place because they had obviously known what to do.

'If only someone had told me, I wouldn't have thrown away the race,' I said to Norman afterwards, with angry tears in my eyes.

As usual he tried to give me a boost. 'You're still learning, Anne. Don't beat yourself up about it. You've learned something valuable from what's happened and that knowledge will help you in the future.'

I knew he was right, but at that moment I wasn't too focused on the positive aspects of having messed up my race.

By the next morning, however, I had realised it would be disastrous to brood on this experience and had vowed to become a stronger racer than ever.

Brian Scobie helped me conduct a post-mortem into the race. He has a huge passion for his athletes. He's very tuned into the tiny aspects that make a good competitor great and believes that hard work can get people a long way. If he can see an athlete is determined to put the work in, he will give a lot of himself to support that person.

We went through the footage together and looked at how the wheels were skidding on the track. It was clear that my equipment had really let me down, but at least I would be prepared if I was faced with similar track conditions in the future.

I continued training hard and reached a different level of pushing. Once again I needed a more up-to-date chair. A local estate agent called Kings Group agreed to support me. One of the partners in the company, a man called Karl, visited me and told me he was impressed by my approach to the sport.

'I can see that you're a very hard-working person,' he said, 'and that it's taken a lot for you to get to this point. You deserve a helping hand.'

He and his colleagues decided they were going to buy me a state-of-the-art chair.

'We're supporting you because I believe everyone deserves a chance in life,' Karl told me. 'I've always grabbed opportunities and I can see that you do the same.'

He came from a humble background, but it hadn't stopped him from developing a very successful business.

I felt very lucky to be offered such a wonderful racing chair, something I could never have afforded myself. It arrived just the day before I flew out to Switzerland for a competition. It was painted yellow to match the Kings Group's logo and I hoped it would be a lucky colour for me. It looked like a work of art to me with its carbon wheels. These can give better power than wheels with spokes. When you put power into wheels with spokes, some of that power gets lost in the spokes.

Switzerland has fantastic tracks and other facilities for wheelchair racers and I knew that I could gain a lot of valuable experience from competing there.

When I got there, though, I burst into tears – my new chair had been damaged in transit and the push rims had buckled. I was devastated. I was feeling fit, all fired up and ready to go – why did this have to happen now? The race was the following day.

I spoke to one of the Swiss advisors and he found a motor mechanic who managed to straighten out the push rims at the eleventh hour. It wasn't perfect, but it would have to do.

Everybody predicted that I would be able to reach faster speeds in Switzerland because of the super-fast tracks. They were right. What's called my top end speed was around 28 kilometres per hour. I couldn't hold that speed for long, but at least I was reaching it and I knew that with more training I would be able to hold it for longer. It was a real breakthrough for me. I was absolutely buzzing with adrenaline and excitement.

When I came off the track, Norman threw his arms around me. He was even more excited than I was. 'Anne, you're flying. Those are the best times you've ever done!'

I knew that I'd moved up a notch.

Wheelchair racers often say to each other, 'What was your top end speed?' I loved being able to reply, 'Twenty-eight kilometres an hour at the finishing line.'

I also loved the way my new chair went so fast and felt as if it was obeying me. I had never had that sort of relationship with a racing chair before.

Wheelchair racing is a long game – it takes time to build up stamina – but I felt that the hours of training I was putting in were starting to yield results. Many of the athletes I met at the Swiss competition were very encouraging towards me too.

I was starting to understand the sport better and the importance of holding top speeds. My times had really improved since I'd started racing. At the Eastern Regional Championships in May 2003 I'd completed the 100-metre sprint in 23.05 seconds. In Switzerland in May 2006 I completed the same race in 18.13 seconds.

As my times improved, I started winning lots of medals. People started to notice me and said I was becoming one of the best female racers in the UK. This was a huge achievement for me and I felt very proud to be representing Great Britain and producing my best work.

I prayed that my new times would be good enough for me to be selected for the world championships in Assen, Holland. This decision would be made by the British Paralympic selection panel. I submitted my new times and hoped for the best.

Soon afterwards I received a letter saying I had been offered a place in the 100, 200 and 400 metres.

I kept on rereading it.

'Yes, yes, yes, I've done it!' I screamed so loudly that I imagine the whole street heard me.

I was absolutely ecstatic. I was getting a taste for big international competitions. I loved the thrill as the adrenaline kicked in when I was pushing to the maximum of my ability. I hoped that I could give the performance of my life on this prestigious world stage. I was determined not to let anyone down.

I phoned my dad and, trembling with excitement, said, 'Guess what? I'm going to the world championships.'

My dad was very proud of my sporting achievements, but nothing mattered to him as much as education.

'Anne, that's very good. I'm happy for you,' he said. 'But when are you going to get on with your MA? You haven't mentioned it for a while.'

Chapter Seventeen

A Bitter Blow

It was a long drive from the airport to the Paralympic village in Assen. When we finally arrived, flags of different nations were fluttering in the breeze. I swelled with pride when I saw the Union Jack and the Kenyan flag. The identities represented by those flags were both part of me.

As I looked around at the other athletes I realised that I was making mental notes about how fit and strong they were rather than wondering what disability they had. It was beautiful to me to see so many athletes together all ready to compete. We were part of an elite, a group that had worked hard and focused on something other than our disabilities.

By the end of the day I could see people laughing and hugging and giving each other high fives. I wondered if they would be acting the same way at the end of the competition. It takes integrity to congratulate someone who has done better than you and to shake them by the hand. However, even though people were very competitive here, I also sensed that there was a lot of generosity of spirit.

I prayed that nothing would go wrong for me this time. I'd trained harder and hopefully smarter than I'd ever trained before, I had a great chair and the weather conditions were good. I was feeling quietly confident when one of the athletes dropped a bombshell, saying it was likely my classification was going to be changed.

I thought it was a joke. I'd been through classification in Athens and been declared a T53 and when I'd first gone in for competitions in the UK, I'd also been classified as a T53. Classification was determined by two physiotherapists and at least one doctor with specialist knowledge of disability, so surely nobody seriously intended to reclassify me now.

Nevertheless I began to hear whispers that I could walk unassisted. If only those rumours had been true! If I'd been able to walk unaided there are so many things I would have done in my life. I would have danced in my waking hours, not in my dreams, for a start. And I wouldn't have had to crawl to the dirty pit latrine at secondary school, I wouldn't have been reliant on family members to carry me on their backs and I wouldn't have had to endure years of pain strapped to callipers and propping myself up with crutches, with all the associated chafing, discomfort, blisters and boils.

I knew that rumours circulate in any community and although I was initially alarmed I tried to dismiss this one. None of the other athletes had grown up with me. They hadn't seen my disability year after year, so perhaps that's why this story had circulated. I also reasoned that polio was an unfamiliar condition to many people and that had perhaps led to a misunderstanding about what I could and couldn't do.

Most members of the British team were disabled following accidents or had cerebral palsy or spina bifida – very different conditions from mine. The only other person on the British team who had had polio was Tushar Patel, a wheelchair racer who had been born in India.

My first race, the 100 metres, was due to start soon, so I tried to put the whole thing out of my mind and focus on my performance.

One of the coaches led us out onto the track and watched us while we warmed up. Then we went into the call room where our numbers, lanes and equipment were checked. I was psyched up and ready to go. I did my first 100 metres in a good time and qualified for the finals. I was delighted.

The finals were scheduled for the following day, so we headed towards the bus that would take us back to our hotel to rest. As we were about to board, the coach received a phone call.

'Anne, you've been asked to go back.'

I was told I had to meet UK Athletics officials. I wasn't unduly worried, though, because I was sure that there had been some mistake. I just hoped the whole thing wouldn't take too long because I wanted to go back to the village to rest in preparation for the finals.

I wasn't told anything and was asked to wait for about an hour before I was finally ushered into an office. There was a doctor from UK Athletics there, a performance manager, a doctor from the International Paralympics Committee and two physiotherapists. I still didn't feel unduly worried. As far as I was concerned, all the evidence of what I could and couldn't do lay in my body and was available to anyone who wanted to find it.

They asked me to perform various movements so that they could assess the level of my disability.

'Could you stand up for us?' one of them said.

'I've never been able to stand up since I had polio,' I replied.

They asked me to do sit-ups, but I couldn't because I didn't have functioning stomach muscles.

They said that they'd been told that I could do both of these things.

The two physiotherapists and the classifying doctor then stayed in the room while I was asked to wait outside with the UK Athletics doctor and the performance manager.

'I don't have a good feeling about this,' I said as the minutes ticked by. After a while they called us in for the results and told me that I was being reclassified as a T54, a more able category.

Feelings of horror flooded my body. I couldn't believe this was happening to me.

'How can life be so unfair? Just when I'm starting to enjoy the sport and really improve at it, it's crumbling in front of me!' I said to myself. 'That sweet dream I had is turning into a nightmare.'

The performance manager said, 'Do you want me to book you a ticket home? I know this isn't an easy thing to handle.'

I looked at her. So many different thoughts were rushing through my mind, but I had worked so hard to get here and there was no way I was going home after only one race. Packing my bags was not an option for me.

'No, there's no need to book me a ticket home,' I replied. 'I've worked and worked to get here. I'm going to go onto that track whatever category I've been put into and I'm going to race to the very best of my ability.'

Now that I had been reclassified, my place in the 100-metre finals was filled by someone else. I felt it was very unjust, but there was nothing I could do about it.

The only race with a vacant slot in the T54 category was the 200 metres, so I entered that. There was no way I was going to quit. I loved racing so much and I was determined to fight on, even though, as I looked at the times of the racers in the T54 category, I knew that mine were nowhere near theirs.

I called Norman.

'I've been reclassified from T53 to T54,' I said in a faltering voice.

'What?' he said. 'Have they given you reasons?'

'Not really. I don't understand why I've been reclassi-fied. Some people seemed to know it was going to happen before I did and that's really hurt me.'

'Are you coming home?'

'No, I'm going to stay and race.'

'That's my girl. I'll support you all the way,' he said.

As we warmed up on the track, I felt as if all the life had drained out of my body. 'Well, all I can do is try,' I said to myself.

I competed in that 200 metres with tears in my eyes. To be honest, I was crying so much that I couldn't even see the lines on the track. I completed the race a broken woman.

After the race one of the athletes said to me, 'You shouldn't have been racing with us.'

That's exactly what I thought.

Not surprisingly, I wasn't in the top eight, so didn't make it into the finals. At least I hadn't come last, though.

I was desperate to get back to the village after that race. I knew I needed to stay strong in public, but all I wanted to do was fling myself on my bed and sob my heart out.

What had happened? Was it racism? Was it that the doctors didn't understand polio, a condition they rarely saw? Was it a genuine mistake? Did somebody have something against me? I had no idea.

Back at the village I saw one of the other competitors.

'I'm so sorry to hear about what's happened, Anne,' she said. 'Are you going to stop racing?'

'Oh no, I'm going to carry on. I'm not a quitter,' I said, taking a deep breath to steady my trembling voice.

'Good for you. Go and relax for a while and then come back stronger,' she said.

I couldn't relax, though. I was struggling to take it all in. 'Why is it all going wrong for me?' I wondered.

The idea that I could be regarded as a cheat was much more wounding than the fact that I'd been reclassified.

All I knew was that some parts of my body didn't work no matter what I did. If I'd been able to make them move I could have cured my disability. The nerves in certain parts of my body hadn't worked since I was two and a half and that certainly wasn't going to change now. I knew I wasn't a cheat and I wondered what I had done wrong.

I returned to England feeling emotionally battered and bruised. But my feelings of utter despair spurred me on. Being pregnant and being a mum to Timothy had taught me patience. Now I was going to need that patience again. I vowed that I was going to train harder than I'd ever trained before and was going to succeed, even if I had been placed in the wrong category. I loved the sport so much and nothing could quench that love.

'Even if it's not my destiny to win any medals in this category, I can still enjoy the racing,' I said to myself.

I began to drive myself even harder in training.

*   *   *

One day I was sitting at home, opening the post. As usual it was mainly bills and circulars, but to my amazement one of the letters was from Buckingham Palace. I had been invited to a reception with the queen in recognition of my work as a disabled athlete and my charity work for people with disabilities.

The invitation said, 'The Master of the Household has received Her Majesty's command to invite Mrs Anne Wafula Strike to a Reception to be given at Buckingham Palace by the Queen and the Duke of Edinburgh on Monday 12th November 2007 at 6 p.m.'

At first I thought it was a practical joke, but Norman assured me it was genuine.

I rushed to phone my dad.

'You're actually going to Buckingham Palace?!' he said. He was so thrilled for me.

When the day of the reception dawned, Norman dressed in his smartest suit and I wore a green trouser suit with African jewellery and beaded braids in my hair. I wanted to look part Western, part African.

We travelled by train to Liverpool Street station and then took a bus to the palace. I'd seen the outside before as a tourist and I felt incredibly excited that I was now going to see the inside too.

'I'm very privileged,' I said to myself.

Inside the palace there were huge paintings and antiques everywhere. I felt as if I was stepping inside British history. I looked at some of the old tables and wondered how many monarchs had used them over the last few hundred years.

We chatted to other members of the public who seemed just as in awe of their surroundings as I was.

After a while an official-looking man came up to us and said, 'Excuse me, would you mind queuing up?'

'What for?' I asked.

'The queen would like to meet you.'

His words made me tremble with excitement.

I wanted to remember every moment of this experience so that I could tell my dad and my family in Kenya all about it.

We queued for a while and then it was our turn to speak to Her Majesty. I felt very nervous, but the queen was good at saying just the right thing. She spoke to me for about five minutes and told me that she herself had enjoyed sport as a younger woman. One of her ladies in waiting asked me which African country I had come from and when I told her Kenya she said that was a country the queen held in very high esteem.

Afterwards we caught the bus back to Liverpool Street station. We were certainly seeing two very different sides of life in one day.

I started travelling all over the world to compete in wheelchair racing events and continued winning medals as a British athlete. My next goal was to get to Beijing for the 2008 Paralympics. Even in my new class of T54 I was determined to make the team.

UK Athletics decided that Jenny Archer should coach me. She had coached wheelchair athletes as young as nine and was very experienced. Alan Stevens continued as my local coach, but I travelled twice a week to be trained by Jenny in London.

A performance coach called Pete Wyman was also in charge of UK wheelchair racers. He travelled around the country and really encouraged all the athletes.

'All you need to do is train, mate,' he said to us.

I'd been preparing for Beijing since Athens. I was so determined to get there and to overcome obstacles like reclassification. We went to qualify in Switzerland and I needed to get 17.25 seconds in the 100 metres to qualify, but my time was 17.37 seconds. My heart sank when I was told I hadn't made the team. If I had been allowed to remain in the T53 category, I would have qualified.

I felt that athletically I was at my peak and that Beijing would have been a great opportunity for me. I was absolutely devastated, but I had no choice but to accept it.

'It's all part of the sport – sometimes you win and sometimes you don't,' I said to Norman, trying to make the best of it.

When my local paper, *The Herald*, found out I wasn't going to be on the team, they asked me to keep a weekly diary about Paralympic sport to raise awareness about it. I continued to feel disappointed that I wasn't competing, but at least with the diary I had some involvement with what was happening in Beijing.

I vowed to continue racing despite my enormous disappointment. I tried to keep my spirits up, but some days I woke up feeling very low. I was particularly upset when I saw that I had done better times in recent races than some of those who had won medals in the T53 category in Beijing.

While competing in a ten-kilometre road race in Australia I crashed my wheelchair and injured my shoulder. I carried on competing for a while, but I had damaged my front deltoid and my rotator cuff. I had to stop training for several months until they healed.

It was hard not being able to train, but my recovery period was a time to reflect on many things. Also, I had developed symptoms of post-polio syndrome. This is when parts of the body affected by polio remember the infection. Due to this condition, I began to experience a tiredness almost like jetlag. I was terrified that I was going to revert to the way I had been when I first contracted polio. But, thank God, it wasn't that bad.

At the end of 2008 the Olympic Medical Institute referred me to Dr Joseph Cowan, a consultant in neurological rehabilitation and neurophysiology, for a medical. He was one of the top polio experts in the UK and sat on the board of the Polio Fellowship. The aim of the medical was to assess the level of my disability.

I had never had a full scientific assessment of my body before and was keen to know what the experts would make of my muscle function. Sometimes when certain muscles don't work, other muscles compensate for them and the body adapts to using these muscles in a different way from those of an able-bodied person.

I arrived at the Royal National Orthopaedic Hospital in Stanmore on a chilly day in December. There was a UK Athletics doctor and a physiotherapist there along with Dr Cowan.

I had no idea what the test would consist of, but was told by Dr Cowan's secretary to prepare for an electromyography test to detect muscle activity. I wasn't sure what this would entail. I felt very apprehensive about it and hoped it wasn't going to hurt.

As soon as Dr Cowan looked at my legs, he said they were typical of someone who had had polio.

I was asked to lie down on the examination couch and to get into different positions. Big long needles were inserted deep into my muscles and Dr Cowan took electrical readings of muscle activity. I shuddered and tried my best to look away so that I couldn't see the needles. The thought of them going deep into me wasn't pleasant.

'It won't take long, Anne, and it will be good to know exactly what's going on in your body,' I said to myself through clenched teeth.

The doctor monitored my muscles for any reaction. I found the whole thing very hard to bear and wondered why with all the advances of Western medicine nobody had come up with a more palatable way to test muscles for responses to various stimuli. I had never had a test like that before and hoped I would never have to go through one again. But I was reassured to be with someone who was a polio expert and looked forward to discovering more about my body.

As the needles were withdrawn, there were spots of blood on the examination table I was lying on. I wasn't keen on the sight of blood and felt quite nauseous. At that moment I intensely disliked the doctors and the physiotherapist. I remembered when I had been treated at the orthopaedic hospital in Nairobi and had been wrapped in plaster for what felt like forever and then strapped into callipers. At that time I had associated doctors with extreme pain. As I lay on the examination table recovering from the test, the same negative emotions about doctors swirled around my brain.

The doctors were talking about what the test had revealed. A lot of what they were saying was medical jargon, but I managed to pick up a few intelligible remarks. 'That's why she can't do a sit-up,' I heard at one point.

I had gone into the test feeling anxious and had come out feeling sore and shaken, but at least now I had a better understanding of how my body worked, which muscles were usable and which bits, no matter what I did, would never change.

'We're sorry to have put you through this difficult test,' Dr Cowan said to me, 'but at least now we know exactly which parts are working and which parts aren't.'

Before I had the test I had known I could do some things and not others, but I hadn't really understood why. Dr Cowan explained that some muscles were compensating for what other muscles couldn't do, but some muscles that didn't work didn't have any muscles that could compensate for them and that was why certain parts of my body didn't work at all.

In his report Dr Cowan said that in the clinical context the picture was compatible with muscles severely affected by old polio: 'The amount of activity seen in the muscles is not likely to give her useful strength in the trunk in my opinion. I would therefore regard her as paralysed below T7.'

I felt sore for a few days after the test, but hoped that now a definitive medical test had been carried out I could be reclassified.

But I heard no more about it.

After being reclassified in Assen I had many dark moments when I considered giving up and walking away from wheelchair racing, but I had never been a quitter and was determined to go out there and show everyone that what drove me forward wasn't how many medals I could win but my love of the sport and the enormous enjoyment I derived from being involved in it. My passion and my bloody-mindedness made me get back into my racing chair and spin round the track. Racing gave me a buzz like nothing else and despite the setbacks I just couldn't bear to give it up. Although I was racing alongside more physically able athletes than myself, I tried my best to filter this out and focus on doing my best.

Even though I struggled in the T54 category, reclassification made me push myself harder than I'd ever pushed myself before. I attended the British squad training camp in Portugal in preparation for the 2007 Paralympic World Cup and experienced an amazing adrenaline rush while I was practising. I just closed my eyes and pretended I was competing in the 400 metres event.

On the morning of the 2007 Paralympic World Cup in Manchester it was pouring with rain. I was feeling very apprehensive and was too nervous to eat breakfast. I just wanted to be called to the start line, hear the start gun and get moving. I wanted to be on my own so that I could completely focus on the race ahead. I kept going to the toilet, something I often did when I was nervous before a race.

We went out onto the track and started warming up. As soon as my wheels started turning, adrenaline surged through me. As I was called to go to my lane I could see that the girls in the other lanes were tough opponents who had achieved great times. If I was to distinguish myself in this race I would have to pull something extraordinary out of the bag. I could hear my heart pounding in my ears. I was wired and raring to go.

When the starting gun went off I pumped my wheels in a way that I had never done before. I was doing well, but when I had almost got to the 300-metre mark, I felt my strength draining away. My arms had turned to jelly.

'I can't go on. I'm so exhausted, I'll have to stop,' I said to myself.

But my determined voice pushed away my defeatist voice.

'Come on, Anne, you can do it. You're almost there.'

My physical strength had diminished, but suddenly I was flooded with mental energy.

'Keep going, move, move,' I silently shouted to my arms and my chair. Somehow I found the strength to get through the last 100 metres.

When I saw that I was the third to cross the line, I was too exhausted to speak. My mouth was dry. I'd used every ounce of everything I had, even my saliva, to get to the finishing line.

'Give me water,' I croaked.

Once I'd revived and recovered, I started smiling and couldn't stop. I couldn't believe that I'd won a bronze medal. I'd proved to myself, and others, that although I'd been knocked down, I'd managed to get up again.

To this day I treasure my achievement in that race above all others. At that moment I felt I really deserved the middle name that my dad had chosen for me. My success in that particularly tough race seemed to be a metaphor for my life. I had been knocked back so many times and I'd often felt that the obstacles in my path were too great to overcome. But from somewhere deep within myself I had found the strength to overcome those hurdles.

After the race my teammates and the crowd congratulated me. Rain had started to fall, but it didn't dampen my enthusiasm. In fact I felt it was a good sign. When something good happens and then it rains, my tribe considers it to be a blessing. I was very proud when I was on the podium with my medal around my neck and I was so happy that I hadn't quit when I was reclassified.

In spite of the pleasure I took in winning that medal, however, winning medals in wheelchair racing has never been the only thing that has mattered to me. Just as important is my journey to the start line and then to the finish line. Travelling is as important as arriving.

Over the years I have grown more comfortable in my own skin. I have begun to understand that the world doesn't owe me anything just because I was struck down with polio. Polio was one piece of bad luck, but I have also had lots of good luck, like a loving family, a good education, a brain that worked well and loyal friends. I have always been determined to prove myself as a hardworking and productive human being and have tried to put every ounce of energy I have into making a success of my life.

My faith in God is strong and I'm convinced that from the time the black mamba snake decided not to bite me that He has been watching over me.

Of course there have been times when I have got angry with God and demanded, 'Why did you decide to make me suffer in this way?' Then I have reminded myself that there are so many people worse off than me. As soon as I have remembered that I have stopped feeling sorry for myself.

I was brought up with a very strong sense of community and the belief that good fortune is something to be shared and not to be claimed by a single individual. If I'm doing well, I want my family and friends and the community around me to be doing well too. We should all be thriving, not just the chosen few.

I'm involved in a lot of different charity work. Previously, as already explained, Norman and I raised money for Machakos School for Physical Disabilities and we are still raising funds to establish a library in my village. We have set up a charity called the Disability Empowerment Association. Our dream is to open a school in Kenya along the lines of Joyland, where disabled children can be given the same opportunities and education I myself was given as a child. The staff at Joyland loved and nurtured us and most of all they believed in us as individual human beings with a contribution to make to the world. They made us believe in ourselves. If we can set up our school in that way, I'll be content.

I'm also a goodwill ambassador for Action on Disability and Development, which promotes a vision of a world where disabled people are able to enjoy their rights and fulfil their responsibilities in the same way as everybody else. I also support Able Child Africa, which supports disabled children and young people in Africa. I also back the Harlow Canal Boat Project, which helps people with disabilities get out and about on the water.

I'm a supporter of the UN Convention on the Rights of Persons with Disabilities and hope that this convention will improve the lot of people with disabilities all over the world.

I also work with local schools to raise awareness about disability and to encourage children of all abilities to believe in themselves and follow their dreams. With hard work and determination, I believe that anything is possible.

Although I feel that I have been incredibly blessed, my life has also been blighted by the tragedy of losing too many people I love.

My first experience of death, when I lost my mum at the age of nine, has had a lasting impact on me. I can still remember the sense of terrible desolation and loneliness that I had when I discovered she was dead. I owe her so much. She showered me with unconditional love and was intuitive about all my needs. She made sure that I could enjoy life despite my problems and surrounded me with a protective bubble of love. She was instrumental in boosting my self-esteem and there is no greater aid to self-confidence than knowing you are truly, deeply loved. I lost my mum too soon, but in the nine years of my life that she was with me she had a huge impact on me.

My oldest brother Ken and oldest sister Alice are gone too. Ken went to a public hospital to get a liver problem treated. His condition was not life-threatening and we hoped that he would make a full recovery, but unfortunately he had to share a bed with another patient. Bed sharing is not uncommon in African hospitals because of a shortage of resources, but it cost Ken his life. The man he was forced to share a bed with had tuberculosis and Ken caught it from him and died of it in 1999 at the age of 34. Tuberculosis is a treatable condition, but in Africa many people die from it because they are unable to afford and access the right treatment. We all loved Ken very much and his death was a terrible blow to us all.

Alice, my beloved older sister, died of meningitis in June 2004, at the age of 42. I felt her loss very keenly because I was very close to her. After my mum died she became like a second mother to me. She often used to talk to me about my childhood and told me many things I had forgotten or never known.

I wish all three were still alive today. I know they would have been very proud of me because all of them knew better than most how I have struggled since the age of two and a half.

Thankfully I still have my dad, my biggest hero. Like my mum, he has loved me steadfastly and has never stopped believing in me and encouraging me. He made sure I received the best possible education and when the villagers told my family to give up on me, he stood up to all of them. I am so happy that I have been able to achieve in many different areas of life and to show my dad the benefits of his love and devotion to me.

Norman and Timothy give me joy every day. My love for Norman is deep and lasting. He has been a tower of strength right from the start and has supported me every inch of the way in all that I've achieved. He makes me laugh so much and every morning when we wake up and start a new day together it's a joy.

Timothy is more precious to me than words can describe. Having been told that I wouldn't be able to have children, I know he is an extra-special gift to Norman and me. He's a happy, well-adjusted boy and is envied by his friends for his caramel skin colour because he always looks as if he's just returned from an exotic holiday. Every time he gives me one of his beautiful smiles, my heart melts. My wish for him is that he grows up to reach his potential in whatever area he wants to excel in. And, like my dad, I want to encourage him to get the best possible education.

I don't know what the future holds for me. I am experiencing symptoms of post-polio syndrome and when I'm tired I start dropping things a lot. It's as if my thumb forgets that it's holding something. At times some movements become more difficult and I get extra aches and pains. The doctors say there's nothing I can do apart from get lots of rest.

But I remain optimistic. I feel that I'm lucky every minute and every second of the day, especially when I see the problems that people with disabilities have in some developing countries.

My hopes are firmly fixed on competing in the London Paralympic Games in 2012. Many of the events will be held not too far from where I live. It's hard to believe that the most prestigious international Paralympic competition in the world is going to be taking place right on my doorstep.

I'm working with my new local coach Ken Day, a man who really knows how to bring out the best in an athlete, and am training as hard as I can in the hope of improving my times. It would be a privilege to be included in the British Paralympic team for 2012.

Wheelchair racing has enriched my life beyond measure. Every time that I get into my racing chair and feel the wind against my face I experience the purest form of happiness. Once my muscles no longer allow me to compete at a high level I hope to remain fit and active and would like to challenge myself by trying other sports like shooting.

I still have so many dreams and aspirations to fulfil. Life is full of new adventures and I'm looking forward to whatever is around the next corner. I feel privileged that I've had a chance to tell my story and hope it will encourage others to take on challenges, believe in themselves and, most of all, when the going gets tough, never ever give up.

End of 2010 edition.

Chapter 18

Haiti

L ike all disabled people, I'm only too aware of the prejudice that we face. I've had so many challenging and upsetting experiences over the years, but I don't think anything could have quite prepared me for the day when people spat on the pavement as they walked past me.

In 2012, I went to Haiti via an organisation called Haiti Hospital Appeal. It was a project that was being run by a young guy called Carwyn Hill. Just two years earlier, Haiti was struck by a devastating earthquake, which killed tens of thousands of people, including so many disabled people, who were more vulnerable because of their disabilities. Another consequence was that it left many people disabled. Of the estimated 800,000 people affected by the earthquake, women and girls with disabilities were among those most impacted. In the aftermath, Carwyn and his wife built a home in Haiti and opened a rehabilitation centre for people with spinal cord injuries.

It was during a conversation with Reverend Gareth Wilde of the Baptist Church that the idea of the trip first came up. I had given a talk about how missionaries had come to Africa and changed my life, and how I really wanted to be a missionary myself at some point. The reverend told me there was an opportunity to go out to Haiti in a charitable role, using my Paralympian background, and make this ambition come true.

When I told him I was interested, he warned me that it would not be a luxury experience. He said I would sleep in a missionary room, have a shared shower and need to cope with just very basic facilities. That wasn't enough to put me off. I was nursing a shoulder injury, so I knew I wasn't going to take part in the London 2012 Games as an athlete. I was in good shape but the triage wasn't working. With the niggle in my shoulder and the classification issue, 2012 would have been a hard call. In truth, the classification blow had hurt me and hurt my athletics career and I would have quit but I decided to continue racing and competing. However, determination can't make you immune to injury. I wasn't going to sit down and complain, so I thought it would be more positive to go to Haiti and train prospective Paralympians of the future.

I saw it as an opportunity to spend time with injured Haitians and encourage them to play sport. Maybe I'd even be able to inspire some to go as far as becoming elite para athletes. For instance, I found out that there was one man with a spinal cord injury who was succeeding at handcyling. He really wanted to be a Paralympian and represent his nation on the world stage. I wanted to help make this happen.

We flew from London, spent one night in Miami and then flew to the Dominican Republic, where we stayed in a lovely resort. The following day, we drove to Haiti. It was a beautiful experience in many ways but going to Haiti was quite another story. The two nations were like two totally different worlds.

It was a four-hour trip to Haiti and even as we were nearing the border, you could start to see the difference setting in. On the Dominican Republic side, it was all well maintained but in Haiti, we immediately saw potholes and broken drainage. We were forced to wait quite a long time before we were cleared to enter the country. Security was very high, and because I was surrounded by three white men I think they found us a suspicious group.

It was extremely hot – hotter even than my motherland, Kenya – and then kids started coming round with trays, selling pancakes made out of mud. I felt so sad when I saw that. Yes, I'm from Africa where poverty's relative, but what I saw in Haiti was frightening. I looked at these kids and thought: they should be in school, not out selling mud cakes, dressed in torn clothes, without any shoes.

But the awful truth was, I hadn't seen anything yet. When other missionaries came to the car and I told them how shocked I was by what I had seen, they said: just wait until you see how bad it is for the disabled population. I could tell there and then that I was going to witness some eye-opening things.

We drove to a hospital where I would be working with disabled people. I would speak with them, encourage them, listen to their stories and then train with them. We were able to identify three people we could potentially open doors for with regards to the London Games. Carywn, who was running the programme, was already in conversation with the International Paralympic Committee (IPC).

Sport is a real enabler: it creates opportunities and it can open doors. We hoped that if these three athletes could compete as Paralympians in London, it would impact how the many Haitians watching at home viewed disability. It was a change that was urgently needed.

The Haitians called disabled people *cocobai*, meaning worthless. Some of the disabled people who lived there told me how bad it was for them. I decided I wanted to experience this for myself. So, with a local disabled man who I was helping to train as part of the Haiti Hospital Appeal Team, I took to the streets. Almost immediately, we noticed that people who walked past us would spit. It was so bad. I broke down in tears. It didn't feel real.

I felt even sadder when someone explained to me that this was actually a relatively mild experience because we looked clean and well dressed. I was told that, if we had been wearing dirty clothes and looked hungry, then rather than spitting to the side, the passers-by would have spat directly on us. I was also told that this was quite an affluent area, and the experience would have been more extreme in other, less well-off areas of Haiti. If somebody can spit at you, how low do you think they regard you? You are completely worthless.

I had so many unforgettable experiences there. One day I was speaking in a children's home, where many abandoned disabled children lived. It was quite a day. I helped to feed the kids, before telling them my own story. I told them about my life in Kenya, how I was born as a normal healthy child and how I contracted polio.

As I told them my story, I broke down crying, because I realised how fortunate I was that my father and mother never gave up on me, despite by disability. Even though the villagers asked my parents to abandon me, they did not. But as I looked at these Haitian kids, I wondered what kind of future they had. These were kids with severe disabilities and no parents. It broke my heart.

Another day, I went to a village where I could speak with mothers who had been persuaded to take back their disabled kids, with the support of the centre. One child didn't have a wheelchair, so the mum had put wheels on a plastic chair, but it had broken. Facing the twin challenges of poverty and raising a disabled child is incredibly tough.

Another experience shook me to my core. One mother got up with her severely disabled child, came towards me and put the child on my lap.

'If you think it's so easy, take her!' she said. 'I don't want this child, so take her!' She told me that every day when she wakes up in the morning, her first prayer is: 'God, I hope my daughter died in the night.' And every evening before bed, she would pray to God to take her child in the night.

I said: 'Why, mama?'

She began to tell me about all the challenges she was facing – and they weren't just practical challenges, she was also facing severe stigma. 'Since I had this disabled child, I cannot get water from the same water station, like the other mothers,' she said. 'I can't just wash my clothes and hang them out like anyone else. I have to hide them because it's a disgrace when you have disability in your home.'

Nobody prepares you for how to deal with a disability; there's no manual. And this mother was deprived. She was a poor single mum with a severely disabled child, who had been shunned by her community. It was so painful to witness her response. And again, this made me really value my mum and dad because they never gave up on me. My dad would say: 'Anne is flesh of my flesh, the blood of my blood. I'm not abandoning her.'

Being disabled is a challenge wherever you are, but Haiti felt like it was 50 years behind Kenya. However, there were positives from the trip. We were able to bring those three athletes to the 2012 Games as wildcards, becoming the first Paralympians from Haiti. Big screens were put up on the streets of Haiti so people could watch these disabled Haitians at the Paralympic Games, and off the back of that, the president of Haiti signed the UN Charter that supports human rights for disabled people. That felt like a real win, as was helping train wheelchair racer Dedeline Mibamba Kimbata, who was awarded an IPC wildcard. She became the first woman from the Democratic Republic of the Congo to race in the Paralympics, and I was so proud to help her.

When I got home, I spent some time reflecting upon the differences between the lives of disabled people in Haiti and here. When we talk about disability, and we talk about empowerment, I look at Britain, which is one of the world-leading nations.

As a world, we need to get to a point where disability is normalised. Where, if you want to get on a train or a bus, you'll just get there because you are a human being. No obstacles whatsoever. At the moment, we hear so much talk about artificial intelligence, when robots will be able to take on all sorts of tasks for us. It seems we'd rather invest in that particular advancement and forget about adapting disabled homes so people can live their lives with dignity.

I am torn about how well we are doing in the UK, because when you look at the progress, questions remain: are we really making progress when some councils are now suggesting that disabled people should be put back in homes to save money? It feels like we've taken 10 steps forward before taking 11 back.

But my trip to Haiti reminded me that, until every nation is making proper progress, we will have to keep fighting for our rights, because we are all in this together. They say that until all are free, no one is free. The same is true here: for as long as disabled people are routinely spat on in the streets in any country, we are all being spat on.

Chapter 19

From the Mud Hut to the Palace

When I was new to the UK, Norman took me to see Buckingham Palace. We looked up at the big, grand palace I had heard so much about and he said: 'This is where the Queen lives.' It was night-time but there were still people outside, taking photographs. How could I have known that one day I would be driven into the palace in a chauffeured car, and that the people outside taking photographs would all turn to look at me? But that's exactly what happened, on the day that the girl from the mud hut became the woman at the palace, accepting an MBE.

I'll always remember when I first found out I was going to be honoured. There I was at home, when this strange-looking letter arrived in the post. It didn't have a normal stamp and I assumed it was some sort of junk mail. So I left it on the table, where it stayed for a while. It's funny to think now that such a letter was just lying there, unopened. Can you imagine that? One of the most important letters of your lifetime, and you don't even open it when it first arrives.

When I eventually read the letter, I couldn't have been more shocked. The person who had written it explained in formal, posh tones that they had the 'pleasure' of informing me that I had been selected to receive an MBE (Member of the Most Excellent Order of the British Empire) for my services to charity and disability sport. I couldn't believe it. I thought: 'Oh my God, this must be a joke!' I rang Norman and told him what the letter said, questioning whether it could be a scam. He was at work, but said he would take a closer look when he got home.

But then I started to get more curious. I noticed the letter gave a telephone number, so I decided to ring it. My heart was pumping as I dialled. When the call was answered, the posh voice at the other end said: 'Buckingham Palace, can I help you?' I was so shocked I just hung up the phone!

Once I realised it was legitimate, I suddenly had a big secret to keep because you're informed not to tell anyone about the award until it goes public. I didn't even tell my son Timothy in case he told his friends and it leaked out. I couldn't tell anyone for nearly three months, which made me feel like such a liar.

Finally, the day came when my name was in the *London Gazette* and the news went public. The whole thing felt like a beautiful dream. I couldn't wait to tell my father, who had always been so interested in British history.

He was so excited and proud, remarking: 'I cannot believe that my daughter who grew up in a mud hut will be going to the palace to be given an award. You're actually going to that big house!'

He was right – it was a really beautiful moment. I'm passionate about working for charity and disabled sports; it never feels like a chore. So, to be honoured for doing the things that I love was so special. Norman was really nice, too. He kept telling me that I deserved it, which was just what I needed to hear.

When news spread, some friends decided they wanted to do something special for me to mark the occasion. They booked us into Grosvenor House on Park Lane for two nights. It's one of the most expensive hotels in London and the lobby alone is enough to take anyone's breath away. They hosted about 150 friends of mine for a meal and reception. I asked my friends why they were doing this and they explained that they'd seen what I do and that I don't expect anything back.

They said I volunteer a lot of my time and money to charitable causes. Even the day before, I had been out competing in a half-marathon, because I was raising funds for a women's disabled group in Africa. When one of the hosts of my reception, Emaka Offor, found that out he made a generous donation, commenting: 'If I was you, I'd have spent today busy doing my make-up and doing my hair.'

Waking up in Grosvenor House on the day I was going to the palace, I thought: This is a good life. I had two really special outfits for the day, because there was no way I was going to dress down for an occasion like this. I had looked for one of the best designers in the world, who would also understand about me being a wheelchair user. With the help of my friend Ruth Clark, I chose a lady from Canada called Izzy Camilleri.

I told her I would like her to make me a dress for a special occasion at Buckingham Palace and she was so excited to help. She said she wouldn't even charge me. She made me two incredibly beautiful outfits: one that I wore to go to the palace, and then another evening gown that I wore for the reception dinner. The morning one had an African theme to it. It was an African fabric, called batik. But I didn't just dress myself, I also dressed my wheelchair, because I wanted to look the part. Everyone said they had never seen anything quite like it.

I arrived in a big chauffeured car with my family and friends. As we swept into the palace, there were hundreds of people outside, taking photographs, just like when I had first visited. As we drove through the crowds I wound the window down and waved at them. I couldn't resist it!

When we got inside the palace, my four guests were taken to one side, and I met my aide for the day. I was shown to a room where we were given refreshments and told exactly how the ceremony would go and what would happen. They told me my name would be called, then I would wheel forward as directed and bow my head because as a wheelchair user I could not curtsey. Then, when the medal was hooked on my dress, I would wheel back, take another bow and sit with my family. They put a hook on my tunic, to make it easier to put my medal there.

My medal was given to me by the Princess Royal, who was wonderful and really took time to talk to me. She complimented me on what I was wearing and my decorated wheelchair, and we spoke about charity. In a whisper, I said to her that I felt so honoured and that this honour was not just for me, but also for the many other African young women, the disabled young women, who can only dream, who never know whether their dreams will become a reality.

My young sister Irene had travelled from Kenya to be there on my big day. When I needed to go to the toilet, my aide for the day couldn't come with me because he was male. Irene and I went to the toilet together, and when we looked at how grand it was, it felt so surreal for both of us. To this day, when she tells people in Kenya that she went to Buckingham Palace they still don't quite believe her.

I fully understand that because it was strange for me, too. I was born in a mud hut. I was ostracised from a village because I contracted polio and became disabled. But on this day, I was in Buckingham Palace receiving an MBE. It just goes to show that even someone from a humble background like my own can achieve so much with God's help. I am blessed.

Chapter 20

Losing Bishar

When my brother Goddard, who we called Bishar, was suddenly taken ill it didn't feel real. He was such an active person and he had never really been unwell. When I found out he was unconscious in hospital, it was such a shock, especially because Bishar had been exchanging messages with friends throughout the day on social media.

He made his final social media post a few hours before he was taken ill. In retrospect, it was an eerie message. Bishar wrote: 'I decided since the sun was taking longer to come out and shine, let me come out, shine and make a change in someone's life. Thanks for the opportunity.'

I had been attending a UK Athletics board meeting as one of the directors. On my way back home on the train, everyone was talking about how the pop star Prince had just died. I was sad and shocked by the news because Prince's music had really inspired me, particularly his famous hit 'Purple Rain'. I love the arrangement of the song and I also enjoyed his vocal performance, including how his vocals explode about two-thirds into the track. That bit feels like accelerating on the track.

When I got home, I plugged my phone in to charge, and my WhatsApp crashed because there were so many incoming messages and calls. I was startled and wondered what was going on. Within a few minutes, I knew. My brother Lopo called on the landline and asked if I had heard the news that Bishar was in hospital unconscious.

I quickly contacted my relatives on the ground back in Kenya. I rang my brother Evans, who was at the hospital along with my sister Vicky, brother-in-law Lawrence and sister Irene. They told me what had happened. Bishar had been at a meeting that evening, and he felt hot and sweaty so asked to get some fresh air. While he was outside, he threw up and lost his balance. They decided to rush him to the nearest hospital, the Coptic Hospital in Nairobi. One of his closest friends used Bishar's car to drive him there and they were joined by another great friend.

I was glad to hear he had friends with him but I was so anxious and agitated back in Essex. I felt even more desperate and frustrated when the hospital staff started dragging their feet. Bishar's blood pressure was over 250 and they were demanding payment before they would admit him properly. In Kenya you have to pay for every-thing at hospitals. The deposit required was KSh 50,000 (roughly £400) but Evans and his team paid KSh 30,000. They spoke with Bishar and said he was coherent. They tried to reassure him and tell him he was in safe hands. He was admitted into the high-dependency unit where they decided to sedate him so they could stabilise his blood pressure. Before long, they moved him to the intensive care unit.

Back in Essex I was asking every question and making every suggestion I could to those in Kenya. The staff told me that a head scan showed very slight swelling on the brain. My immediate concern was to get a neuro-surgeon to look at the scan and recommend treatment as an emergency. Time was of the essence and if Bishar was to have a chance to pull through, there could be no margin for error or time wasting.

I told the family that a neurosurgeon needed to see Bishar urgently. I told them to insist. It was getting late and the chances of my brother surviving were diminishing by the minute. I went online to try to find a neurosurgeon but the hospital said only their resident neurosurgeon would be allowed to see Bishar. But where was the neurosurgeon? They said he was in the hospital but then I found out this wasn't true. Within an hour, the hospital staff were demanding the outstanding deposit and payment for that day. It felt heartless.

My sister Jane asked the doctors and staff if my brother was responding to the medication. One staff member let her tongue loosen and said they don't switch off the life-support machine suddenly; they do it gradually. Jane was shocked by her words but then she was quickly reassured that everything would be okay. What was going on? If everything was going to be okay, then where had this talk of the life-support machine being switched off come from?

I tried my best to remind myself that Bishar was one of life's fighters and so many times when I've faced challenges in life, he's reminded me that tomorrow is a new day. I also turned to Bible verse for comfort: Psalms 62: 'Let all that I am wait quietly before God, for my hope is in Him.' I continued to speak to relatives, to find out more information and to give what advice I could. I also booked an air ticket to fly to Nairobi.

I was told Bishar had suffered a stroke and straight away I started to create a plan of care for him. I thought, he'll be in hospital for a while and when he wakes from the coma he might struggle with speech and coordination. He might need a wheelchair and a walking stick, while he recovered.

As a wheelchair user, I believed we could have a satisfactory support plan in place. I heard success stories about people who had recovered from strokes and I wasn't going to my write my brother off. We were going to fight this together. Those were my thoughts at the end of that unimaginable day. But the next day would be far, far worse.

It actually started quite well, with family streaming in to visit Bishar. I managed to get the neurosurgeon on the phone and I poured out all of my frustration to him, expressing my disappointment at the shocking quality of care given to my brother. The neurosurgeon did not sound sympathetic or even bothered and he asked me to call him an hour later.

Then I heard from my sister Irene, who had been in to visit Bishar. She said that when she held his hand and touched his arm, she felt no pulse and she quickly alerted Uncle Peps who was in the room with her.

When I spoke to my brother Arthur, my heart sank, because all he said was: 'Where are you? Come quickly! Bishar has left us. Come quickly, he's gone!' He was choking over the phone and holding back tears. I quickly hung up because that was not the news I wanted to hear. After a few minutes, I rang my cousin and demanded one answer from him: I asked if it was good or bad news. He replied: 'Bad.' But still, I was unable to accept what I was hearing.

I rang my sister Jane, who was wailing and asking God many questions. I then received a text from my dad, which read: 'Cancel your journey. He is dead.' My heart sank, I felt dizzy and sick. I didn't know where to look. I felt like all my insides would all come out.

Bishar had passed away at noon. I spoke to Evans, who was devastated too and totally broken. Evans told me he was the last person to speak with Bishar as they reassured him he would get well. He was alert and communicating before the sedation. Evans told us that when Bishar was sedated, he started to sing a hymn as he slipped away. It was his favourite hymn and was the ringtone on his phone, too. As fate had it, the words of the hymn were also the final ones he ever uttered on this earth:

Kaa nami ni usiku sana (Abide with me; fast falls
    the eventide)
Usiniache gizani bwana (The darkness deepens;
    Lord with me abide)
Msaada wako haukomi (When other helpers fail
    and comforts flee)
Nili pekee yangu, kaa nami (Help of the helpless,
    O abide with me)

My kid brother left a very big impression on all of us. He also left behind three children. What a tragedy. I didn't grieve at first because there was so much going on. I went to Kenya to bury my brother, but it wasn't until I got back to the UK that the grief hit me. I sometimes wonder: did Bishar somehow know he was about to leave us, even before he fell ill? When I spoke with friends of his, lots of them said that he sent them messages around that time. And then he sent that final Facebook post, which ended: 'Thanks for the opportunity.'

Rest well, dear brother.

Chapter 21

Speaking Out

I've been one to speak out for as long as I can remember. My dad tells me that even when I was young, when things weren't going well, I used to demand that we have a family meeting to discuss it. I'd say, 'I'm not happy with the way my brother treated me', or raise anything else I was concerned about.

Because of his role in the army, sometimes my dad would be gone for weeks or months at a time. One time I called a meeting to say I wasn't happy that he had to keep going away because we missed him. I was really young, and I was trying to demand that he came home every weekend, but because of his job he couldn't.

My dad was a great fan of me speaking up at those family meetings – he enjoyed how I challenged my siblings. His mother, my paternal grandmother, was certainly a strong, tough woman. She was outspoken, and an activist in a way, because she called out an injustice when it happened in the village. She never took any rubbish from anyone. She believed no one should become a slave of another and everyone should be free. She used to say to me that when I grew up, I'd meet people from different walks of life – and that when you're fighting for something you really believe in, you have to stand strong, like a baobab tree, which are big, sacred trees in Africa.

When you're an activist or a campaigner, if you fall down, you just want to fall like the seeds that still grow up and produce so many baobab trees. So that way, our activism is never in vain. Sometimes you win the cause you're fighting for, and sometimes you don't. But you never *fail* if you sow seeds. I look at all the people we've brought on board to talk about the issue of disability and how we've planted that seed into their lives and their hearts. That seed is going to grow and germinate. So even when I'm not here, in decades to come, these are the people who are going to carry on the work that means so much to me. This is why I will keep speaking out, no matter what cost it is to me.

A good example of this is what happened to me on a train one day. I'd gone to a town called Corby, in Northamptonshire, overnight for a meeting with UK Athletics. The meeting was really positive. We discussed strategy and I talked about inclusion and how we can help people with disabilities access athletics.

It had been a good meeting, with my suggestions getting a positive reception, so I was feeling really upbeat when I left to get the train home. I was in what they call the accessible carriage but because they had put me next to the window, I couldn't see whether the toilet door was opening and closing, so there was nothing to suggest to me that the toilet was out of order.

Halfway through the journey, I needed to use the toilet. But when I went to open the door, it wasn't opening. There was a female guard on board so I explained the situation. She said: 'Oh, I'm so sorry, it's not working. It's out of order.' But no one had told me this when I was getting on the train.

She asked me how quickly I needed to go. I told her I really needed to. She said: 'Okay, what I'm going to do is, we'll try the next stop, then we will get you out and hold the train so that you can go and use the toilet in the station.'

She agreed that they should have told me the toilet was out of order before they put me on the train, so they would wait while I used the station's toilet, as it was their mistake. But when we got to the station, they couldn't get me off the train because the station wasn't manned. That meant that disabled access was also closed because they needed somebody to help get me through the barriers, and there was nobody there.

So we agreed to try the next station. But that didn't work either, because there were no wheelchair facilities and there was no lift. I would have needed to go up the steps, and then climb down the steps, which was not feasible for me. They suggested we try again at the next stop, Leicester.

Meanwhile, I had also been speaking on Twitter, now known as X, with the train company and they had suggested I get off at Peterborough station, use the toilet there and then they would arrange for a taxi to take me home. I agreed with this and gave them my postcode but by now the wait had become just too much for me. I couldn't hold it any longer and I wet myself.

I could feel it coming and I thought: 'You can't do this, because you're not a toddler, you're a grown woman.' I don't normally struggle with incontinence, so why should I wee myself? It was like a slow-motion movie where I couldn't hold it anymore. I just put my head in my hands, thinking: 'Oh my God, this is just so unfair.' In that moment, I felt so disabled, so excluded, because using a toilet is a basic right. I'm sure you consider it a basic right, too.

When I was growing up, I never thought that something like this would happen to me – especially in a developed nation. There's no way I'd have believed I would pee myself in my wheelchair here. When you're growing up in Africa, you believe that Britain treats their disabled and their vulnerable people with respect and care. I had a lot to learn.

When they got me off the train, I was crying so I covered my face with a hoodie because I was worried people would recognise me. I was so embarrassed. I couldn't move my wet cushion. I had to sit on it until I got home.

Things were about to get even worse. There was no taxi at the station. I told them my body was aching and I was sitting in my own urine in my wheelchair. I don't think they really understood how demeaning it is for a grown woman to wee herself on a train and then have to wait around on a platform in the cold in her soiled clothing. Where's the respect and human dignity? I said I felt like throwing myself under one of their trains.

As soon as I got back to the house, I flung myself on the bed and sobbed. I put my cushion by the radiator, so it could dry off. Then I had a shower and sprayed myself with perfume.

Obviously, this was a really embarrassing incident for me. It was horrible, but I was determined to highlight it, so I made contact with a journalist. I told her my story and explained that I would like to go public about it because I was afraid that if nothing was done, the problem would continue.

Once the article went live on the *Guardian*, the news spread far and wide and a lot of people contacted me to discuss it further. Many people would be too embarrassed to talk about it. But I wasn't doing it just for my own good, I was doing it for the good of other people. But I went all in and did a lot of campaigning on this specific issue, going on TV and radio, doing everything I could because I knew what had happened was ableism. It was an experience that really disabled me and did not allow me to be a full human being.

As soon as the articles were published, people left

comments and sent emails, saying that the same thing had happened to them. Many disabled people and even parents with disabled children said: 'This has happened to us.' Some had even ended up quitting university because the toilets were so often out of order that they would be caught short. In some ways, I felt frustrated that no one had gone public before, but it helped confirm I'd done the right thing in speaking out myself.

Shockingly, some of the responses to the articles were along the lines of: 'Well, you're from Africa. At least here we have disabled toilets.' But what they don't know was that if I was in Africa, there's no way I would have wet myself. I travelled on buses in Africa, and if you were doing a long journey, the drivers used to stop every hour or so, to let people use the toilet.

Or sometimes if a passenger wanted to go and relieve themselves, you would just tap the driver or the ticket conductor and say: 'I want to use the toilet.' You would go behind a bush or some trees. We never wet ourselves. People would have carried me from the bus, and taken me behind a tree.

Some people said to me: 'Why are you even talking about such an embarrassing experience? Don't you want to be known as a glamorous Paralympian? If you talk about these things, people will know you as that lady who had an accident on the train.' I say to them that what happened on the train could happen to other disabled people too. Whether I'm a Paralympian or not, I need to speak out for them.

It's true that it would have felt easier not to speak publicly about such an embarrassing and personal incident. But I didn't want it to happen to me again and I didn't want it to happen to any other person in my situation in the future, either. Just because I have a disability it does not mean that I am available for this kind of humiliation. Having access to a toilet is a basic human right and being denied it in this century was like a bad dream.

When it happened to me, it robbed me of my dignity, which I've worked for many years to build. It's been a lot of work to reach a stage where I love myself, despite the fact that I'm a wheelchair user.

It made me feel so invisible, like nobody cared. But speaking out empowered me again and it put the issue on the table, forcing the government to speak about it publicly. Recently, the government has allocated more than £30m for the provision of Changing Places toilets but more needs to be done.

It's not that I particularly *enjoy* speaking out. But I don't have the luxury of choosing, or of it being a decision. I think governments tend to choose when to play the disabled card to favour them, and when to throw them under the bus. And we saw that during the pandemic. It felt like a reality check: one moment there was the euphoria of the London Paralympics 2012, when society looked at disabled people with amazement at what we could do when we were given an opportunity. We became household names and deep-rooted negative beliefs about disabled people were challenged.

But then suddenly Covid happened and we were back to the harsh reality. Because the reality of the pandemic for disabled people was terrifying. Disabled people were afraid to go to hospital when they contracted Covid because it was not guaranteed that they would get oxygen or the treatment they needed. There were tiers for who would get what level of treatment. In other words it was a real-life example of that chilling idea: the survival of the fittest.

If you were disabled and you caught Covid, you were put in a different tier than non-disabled people when it came to treatment. It was as simple and cold-blooded as that.

Finding out that disabled people were being asked to sign 'do not resuscitate' forms was so scary. We were seen as the weak link in society. It felt like they were saying: well, we can throw these ones under the bus. They can be the first to go because if they die that would free up a bed for somebody else who may make more money for society.

During Covid, we were all given a financial value, so it was the most profitable people who were put in the top tier for treatment. That's what it comes down to. As part of a marginalised group, I already knew a gap was there: the gap between the haves and the have-nots, between the rich and the poor. But that gap became so much bigger to me during the pandemic.

Some days I would sit in my house so frightened: what if I now get Covid and I need that oxygen? I'll go to hospital with a 'do not resuscitate' form and I will die because I have a disability. I won't be given a chance to survive.

We saw that gap again when the government started opening things up, when their focus was to bring money back into the economy. It didn't seem to bother them how the reopening would affect vulnerable or disabled people. We could go to the galleys as far as they were concerned.

It was horrific. They said everybody could just get on with life, without really bringing in the right measures to support the disabled. At the start of the pandemic they had told us to 'shield' first, but when it came to reopening, they didn't tell us: don't come out too quickly. We were scared and confused. Why was it suddenly okay or safe for us just to go out?

I remember speaking to a friend who has a disability and she had not left the house for a long time. At the point when everything was reopening suddenly, she wondered whether all that sacrifice had been in vain. Maybe we should have just gone out, perhaps contracted Covid and died, because it seemed like not a lot had been done to protect the vulnerable.

My family and I had taken cover together at home. I'd hoped that the world or nation might have behaved like a family, where you look after the people around you. But instead there was this stampede for people to go out.

I decided I wanted to speak out, so I wrote an article for the *Guardian*, saying that a caring society would have made disabled people a priority, but instead, from the very beginning of the pandemic, disabled people were treated as an add-on.

I invited the readers to imagine how it felt to be stuck in the house for two years with little or no social contact because of your disability or vulnerability. For many disabled people, the only human they had interacted with was their carer, the person delivering post or food. Or they might have an occasional wave through the window to family members. It's so chilling to look back at how the pandemic affected everyone's lives, but for disabled people it was particularly painful. At one stage, six out of ten deaths from Covid in the UK were those with disabilities.

Sometimes people think that when you're campaigning for disabled rights, you are encouraging laziness, but that's not what we're aiming for at all. I campaign because I know how useful every individual is and that they can each contribute in their own different ways.

A better way to empower disabled people would be to create opportunities for them, not drag them to do something that might be inappropriate. So that's why I advocate for inclusion, because when you are including someone with a disability and making it possible for them to contribute, that's much better than trying to force them to contribute in a manner that they are not able to.

These issues have showed themselves clearly during the cost-of-living crisis, too. It's been a really challenging time for everyone, including disabled people. Again, we were made to feel like we were being blamed for the problems the country was experiencing. When the cost of living shot up, some disabled people flagged they would need a bit more help and support, which many in society rejected the idea of.

I saw my heating bills going up, because I needed to have my heating on for longer while I was spending more time in the house. So it was a challenge. But I knew that if it was a challenge for me, then it would be affecting other disabled people even more. I spoke to some other disabled people who were struggling too.

One mum told me that she had to choose between switching on the machine that keeps their child alive or having the heating on. That really shocked me. Another family had given up using a washing machine, and turned off their heating in all the rooms apart from the room of their disabled child. What does that tell you about society and our views on disability in such a rich nation?

Speaking out comes with a price but I've amplified other people's voices. Disabled people are realising that it is okay to speak up when things are wrong. I've helped empower them so they know it is not embarrassing to speak about the issues that affect us. This, to me, is spreading the baobab seeds, just like my grandmother taught me.

Some disabled people, who don't have as high a profile as Paralympians, might think that they can never achieve what we have achieved and therefore they might not have the confidence to speak up. This is wrong. Meanwhile some Paralympians I know of, who wanted to become activists and campaigners, thought they might not look as good on camera as some of the people they see in the media. They lacked confidence in other ways, too. I always say: it's not about how one looks, it's not about how one sounds, it's about the passion one has to create change. And if you really want to change something, you can do it and you can do it in your own authentic way.

Never underestimate your power. We can all advocate for fairness and equality in society. Some of us are campaigners, some of us are activists, some of us are lobbyists, some of us are educators. We challenge misconceptions in different ways. Passion is more important than a polished presentation.

When I speak up in my strong African accent, I may speak differently to people who were born and bred in this country. But I am not trying to be one of them: I am a citizen of the world, I have seen the need for change and I believe there can be a better world, with equality, inclusion and equity.

And we should never give up, because it took me a long time to find a voice. But now that I've found it, I'm not going to be silenced any time soon.

Chapter 22

That's My Son!

It was such a proud day for me and Norm when our son Timothy graduated from the University of Hertfordshire as a Bachelor of Science in Sports Science. This is the child that I prayed to God for. This is the child for whom, when I was expecting him, I was told I must have a termination. Imagine if I had listened to those doctors at the time. It hardly bears thinking about. And here Norm and I were. More than 20 years on, watching him graduate from a British university.

He had extra obstacles to overcome to get there because he had been studying during the Covid pandemic, which disrupted so many young people's education. He and I made the most of the challenges of the pandemic. We turned our garden into a small gym, so we were training and exercising every day.

Covid proved to be a big bonding experience for us but there was no hiding from the effect it had on his education. Sometimes the classes were in person and sometimes online. On some days, he would turn up and the tutor wasn't there. It was really tough for him and he had so much work to do amid all the disruption. So I'm incredibly proud that he made it.

Timothy is my biggest joy, my biggest supporter and my biggest campaigner. It's natural for a child to look up to their parents but now I also look up to him. And I've never been more proud than I was on the day he graduated from university.

I was so excited I could have burst. When he stood up to get his degree, I made that famous African ululation sound. And I shouted: 'That's my son! That's my son!' When he passed me to go back to where he was sitting, because I was at the aisle, he stopped and did a small dance and we high-fived.

Life felt amazing in that moment and the day was a blessing. It was miraculous when I brought Timothy into the world. I am blessed to be his mother and he also says he feels blessed that he is my son. My life has had so many ups and downs – it's been quite a journey. But being a mother feels like the biggest blessing of all.

Acknowledgements

S o many people have helped and supported me on my
journey and I would like to say a big thank you to
them all.

My late mother nurtured, loved and protected me
during the first nine years of my life, along with my dad
and my sisters and brothers.

My teachers at school and university believed in me
and generously encouraged me, while my friends
laughed and cried with me and helped me with basic
tasks like fetching water, things I was unable to do for
myself.

I also owe an enormous amount to my coaches, who
have stood shivering on race tracks in the depths of
winter urging me on. Without all of you I would not be
where I am today.